10-
2M

THE NOTEBOOK OF AN AMATEUR POLITICIAN

To my Parents
Agent. I hope
she enjoys the book

6/20/2

Margot and Gilbert Hahn, Jr.

THE NOTEBOOK OF AN AMATEUR POLITICIAN

(And How He Began the D.C. Subway)

Gilbert Hahn, Jr.

LEXINGTON BOOKS
Lanham • Boulder • New York • Oxford

The article *Meeting House Farm Is Winning Combination* by Lucy Acton found on pages 53–56 was first published in *The Maryland Horse* (January 1988). Reprinted with permission.

Cover photograph © 1985 The Washington Post. Photograph by Gerald Martineau. Reprinted with permission.

LEXINGTON BOOKS

Published in the United States of America
by Lexington Books
An Imprint of the Rowman & Littlefield Publishing Group
4720 Boston Way, Lanham, Maryland 20706

12 Hid's Copse Road
Cumnor Hill, Oxford OX2 9JJ, England

British Library Cataloguing in Publication Information Available

Library of Congress Cataloging-in-Publication Data

Hahn, Gilbert, 1921–
  The notebook of an amateur politician : and how he began the D.C. subway / Gilbert
Hahn, Jr.
    p. cm.
   ISBN 0-7391-0405-5 (pbk. : alk. paper)
     1. Hahn, Gilbert, 1921– 2. Politicians—Washington (D.C.)—Biography. 3. District of
Columbia City Council—Biography. 4. Washington (D.C.)—Politics and government—1967–
1995. 5. Washington (D.C.) Politics and government—1995–
6. Washington (D.C.)—Biography. 7. Subways—Washington Metropolitan Area—History. I. Title.

F201.3.H34 N68 2002
975.3'041'092—dc21
[B]

                                                                                    2002023568

Printed in the United States of America
The paper used in this publication meets the minimum requirements of American National
Standard for Information Sciences—Permanence of Paper for Printed Library Materials,
ANSI/NISO Z39.48–1992.

To Margot, with love

Contents

ഓരു

Foreword

ⅎ⅋

In my account of the 1965 election campaign of John Lindsay for mayor of New York, I relate how Robert Sweet, later a judge but then a lawyer and Lindsay's campaign manager, sent me to the Lindsay headquarters at 125th Street in Harlem on the day of the election.

When he'd finished briefing me, Bob pressed a thick wad of twenty-dollar bills into my hand and told me it was "election day money." When I got back to headquarters at the end of the day, I dutifully returned the entire wad. Only later did I learn that I was supposed to have spent what needed to be spent and pocketed the rest.

Hence my title, *The Notebook of an Amateur Politician.*

Acknowledgments

ഩരു

Thanks to John Greenya for his help in editing this notebook, as well as my special thanks to Jim Lyons of Rowman & Littlefield, as well as Martin Hayward of Lexington Books.

Introduction

ഔ

Early Days in Washington

B ack in 1921, the year I was born, Washington was still a small town, and, in many ways, also a hick town. Believe it or not, in those days the Big City was Baltimore, our neighbor to the north. It had many wealthy people, socially accepted people, and good-sized businesses. If you wanted anything of importancc in thosc days you had to go to Baltimore to get it.

A good hospital? Washington didn't have one, but, then as now, Baltimore had Johns Hopkins. Need to borrow more than $10,000? No bank in Washington would lend you that much, but several Baltimore banks would. And if you were an intellectual, you eschewed the Washington papers in favor of the *Baltimore Sun*. When you were older, if your tastes were on the "raffish" side, the night spots you frequented were in Baltimore, not Washington.

For members of the Jewish community in Washington, being invited to a party in Baltimore was the height of acceptability.

If you were a newcomer to the USA, an immigrant bound for Washington, Baltimore was your port of entry, your Ellis Island to the south.

When I married Margot shortly after World War II, her friends commiserated with her. What a shame that she would have to leave Baltimore for déclassé Washington. But things have a way of changing, and over the years the pecking order has changed and Washington is now on the top rung, with Baltimore below it. I knew things had changed some years ago when Margot started telling people that if we ever divorced she would get to keep Washington.

*   *   *   *   *

What follows, though not necessarily in chronological order, is a personal account of what has transpired, both to Washington and to me, in those years since I first appeared on the scene. Because certain events were beginnings, I have used them to organize these memoirs, or, to use the term I prefer, this *notebook*. They include my life and good times in politics, the wonderful and sometimes strange personalities I have had the fun of meeting and in some cases working with, tales having to do just with the District of Columbia, whose fellow citizens I've been privileged to serve in several capacities over the years, and then my own little war stories.

    I beg your indulgence, and hope that you enjoy these pages from my notebook.

Chapter 1

ഇൗൽ

D.C. Matters

How I Began the Subway (part 1)

Congress never really intended for Washington to get a subway. The carrot of a subway was held out as a bribe in order to get the city to complete the interstate highway system.

The "military industrial complex," which we've all heard so much about, was a little thing compared to what was involved in the building of the interstate freeway system.

During his administration, President Eisenhower started the interstate freeway system modeled on the Autobahn that he'd found in Germany during the war. Gasoline was taxed so many cents per gallon, which built up into an autonomous fund containing billions of dollars. In addition to the money, the interests that were involved in completing the freeway system were enormous, vast, powerful. They included all the automobile and truck manufacturing companies; all the gas, oil, steel industries; and the unions, like the Teamsters, that had to do with transportation. It was a very powerful group. When I came to the City Council in 1969, the people whom I have described, who were involved in seeing that the highway system was completed, had become frustrated over the opposition of city residents around the country who didn't want the interstate system to come through their cities. One of those cities in opposition was Washington, D.C.

Much of the power of the freeway complex was centered in the chairman of the Public Works Committee of the U.S. House of Representatives. Members of the interstate freeway complex and Congressman Dan Rostenkowski got together and made up their minds that, "Goddamit, if there was one city in the country that the Congress controlled that was Washington, D.C.," and they were damn well going to complete the interstate system through the District of Columbia.

The plan was to complete: the beltway; the inner beltway; the north central freeway; and, most important of all, the Three Sisters Bridge to carry I-95 south through Washington. Mayor Walter Washington and Deputy Mayor Tom Fletcher had already been put on notice by the chairman of the Public Works Committee (and their catspaw) Congressman Natcher of Bowling Green, Kentucky, chairman of the House subcommittee on the District of Columbia budget. They were directed to complete the interstate freeway system through Washington and the Three Sisters Bridge, and if they did so they had been promised that the Congress would fund a subway system for the District. As I had guessed, and came to find out, the Congress and the interstate highway complex in fact had no intention of ever funding a subway system for the District of Columbia.

My office, as chairman of the City Council, was on the fifth floor of the District Building at one end, as was the City Council's office, and at the other end the office of the mayor and deputy mayor. On the first day I took office, Tom Fletcher called and invited me into his office for a talk.

He began with the words, "Gil, there's this bridge." He said that there was a bridge called the Three Sisters Bridge that, after the freeways had been constructed, would take traffic through the city of Washington and across the Potomac River below Georgetown at a trio of islands known as the Three Sisters. The Three Sisters Bridge would carry I-95 into Virginia, thus continuing the freeway system south to Richmond.

Tom Fletcher explained that it was all organized, all set up and arranged that "we," the City Council, would agree to complete the North Central Freeway, the Inner Beltway, and several other interstate road systems in and through the District of Columbia, but most particularly the Three Sisters Bridge. Tom said it was all set with Congressman Natcher, Congressman Rostenkowski, and the Public Works Committee. As chairman of the City Council, having inherited the power of the former Engineering Commission, I had the final say as to where roads went, and would be the one to sign off on the system. Once I had done that, it was explained to me, then Congress would vote us the money to begin the subway system.

The key to it, according to Tom, was that I was to execute a statement that the mayor's corporation counsel, Charlie Duncan, had prepared, saying that I found I had no power over roads and freeways in the District of Columbia. Then the mayor and Tom Fletcher would take it from there, build the Three Sisters Bridge, and complete the interstate freeway system. Hmmm.

I went to the other end of the hall and sat down in my brand new office and thought all this over. I was quite aware that the office that I inherited under its prior leadership of the City Council actually did nothing at all with the City Council. Certainly they passed no legislation and held no legislative hearings; but they did issue the occasional proclamation and generally acted as a cheering section for Mayor Washington.

I thought about all this because I had the notion to turn the City Council into a real legislative body enacting real budgets, holding real hearings and investigations, actually acting on the city budget and its taxes, and it didn't take long to see that announcing that I had no powers over the Three Sisters Bridge and the rest of the interstate freeway system in the District of Columbia would doom my plans.

I went back and told Tom Fletcher that I didn't agree to do what he had wanted. This was followed of course by promises by Tom Fletcher that the sky would fall on my head, and various dire threats, plus the issuance of a very nasty statement by Charlie Duncan.

All of this firmed my resolve. During my term in office I would not complete the interstate freeway system through the District of Columbia. And I wouldn't build the Three Sisters Bridge. But I *would* build the subway system.

I very quickly found out what it meant to be at the business end of the anger of the interstate freeway complex, or, as they were also known, the "freeway lobby." I guess I heard from thousands whose attitude can be summed up as, "Who is this son of a bitch Hahn who is against freeways?"

Both the *Evening Star* and the *Washington Post* weighed in with hostile editorials against my decision not to build the freeway system. This was certainly understandable as both newspapers had built expensive printing plants in the city and were planning to make use of the interstate system to deliver their papers more easily.

The only voice of reason at the time was Mayor Washington, who spent a good deal of time coaxing me to change my mind. Arrayed against the freeway lobby was a fiercely vocal, but not very impressive, group called the Emergency Committee for the Transportation Crisis. This was a group headed by an otherwise very nice young man named Reginald Booker and included Sammy Abbott, former Communist candidate for the House of Representatives from Buffalo and later the mayor of Takoma Park. It also included Julius Hobson and, as one of the chorus, Marion Barry. I held some freeway and Three Sisters Bridge hearings, which immediately broke up into several famous riots (but more of that later.)

The committee was funded by solid citizens of Georgetown like attorney Ed Burling. Their interest in the matter was to prevent the Three Sisters Bridge—or any highway—through Georgetown, and so they funded Reginald Booker and all of his confreres very lavishly. When a hearing on the Three Sisters Bridge broke up in yet another riot, I had Ed Burling and his fellow Georgetowners to thank for paying Booker and Company to riot. Among other things, I was hit with a flying ashtray.

Why was I so adamant? I don't give myself any particular merit badges for agreeing with the argument that freeways would ruin the city and Balkanize its different parts by putting up a "Chinese Wall" through the middle of a neighborhood. It's just that I thought that it was a good thing not to have the freeways and the Three Sisters Bridge, and a better thing if I could manage to get the subway system funded instead.

In 1969 the mayor had put $200 million into the city budget for the beginning of the subway. The mayor and I both dutifully attended hearings before Natcher's committee, the subcommittee of the House Appropriations Committee for the District of Columbia. The year before, Mr. Natcher, in leige to the Public Works Committee, had removed the subway money from the budget, sent the amended budget to the House floor, and the House promptly passed the budget minus the subway money.

I asked for help from Daniel Patrick Moynihan, who was then President Nixon's counselor for domestic affairs and whose duties included taking charge of the District of Columbia. His comment was, "Gil, you run the city of Washington. Take charge of it and don't bother me." After several other equally "helpful" conversations at other levels of the president's cabinet and counselors, I went to see my old friend Attorney General John Mitchell.

Though he liked to hide the fact, John Mitchell liked cities, was interested in their problems, and knew a great deal about them. He agreed with me not to put in the freeways and the Three Sisters Bridge, and he said he would help me get the money to start building the subway system.

One day not long after that, Mitchell sent for me. He told me to go see Secretary of Transportation John Volpe, the former governor of Massachusetts. I met with Volpe and his marvelous administrative assistant, Joe Bosco.

Soon after that meeting, Joe called me and said, "Gil, Secretary Volpe has it in his power to lend the Subway Authority $200 million to get the subway system started. We understand that's the amount of money you need. However, we'll need to get clearance on this at the White House." Whether or not the president gave his approval to Volpe's plan to lend the Subway Authority $200 million was placed in the hands of a young White House staffer by the name of Egil "Bud" Krogh.

We sat in a small conference room somewhere in the White House executive offices. We knew that Krogh was in the next room, and somebody (we didn't know who) was opposing the lending of the $200 million for the subway was in the third room, on the other side of Krogh. Krogh went back and forth, listening to our arguments as to why the president should authorize this, and then he went to talk to the unknown group who were there opposing the loan of the money. After two hours of this back and forth Krogh came into our room, shook our hands, congratulated us, and said he had decided to recommend to the president that the money be lent to the Subway Authority.

We came into the hall together and then we saw that it was General Graham, head of the Subway Authority, and some of his top staff who had been in the other room opposing the $200 million loan. Graham was so angry that he came up to me, began to cry, and startled me by grabbing me by my lapels and shaking me. "Hahn," he said, "you're interfering with my mission, which is to build freeways."

I realized after that that General Graham had been appointed to his post (he had been a Corps of Engineers general) by the Public Works Committee, and his job as head of the Subway Authority really was to see to the completion of the interstate freeway system and the Three Sisters Bridge. Nevertheless, the president duly authorized Secretary Volpe to lend $200 million to General Graham and the Subway Authority to get the subway started, and the money was duly made available to General Graham and the Subway Authority. However, the other side had the last laugh (at least for a while). General Graham and the Subway Authority refused to spend the money, so for the rest of the year, nothing happened. (Although no one knew it at the time, Egil "Bud" Krogh was then the head of the Plumbers, who were looking for leaks in the basement of the White House. He would later go to jail for these activities.)

How I Began the Subway (part 2)

History repeated itself the next year. Congressman Natcher and the Budget Committee repeated its cycle. Once again, $200 million or so was put into the city budget to start the subway system, and once again Congressman Natcher vetoed the item. However, this year, a possible hero appeared in the person of a junior member of Congressman Natcher's committee who proposed an amendment to the city budget to be acted on the floor of the Congress to restore the money. The name of this white knight was Don Giaimo of Connecticut.

At that point, I went to Congressman Hale Boggs, a man who had always been a lovely and generous friend to Margot and me. I asked him if he would be willing to support Congressman Giaimo's amendment to the budget on the floor of the House, and he surprised me by saying yes he would indeed do that, but only if he thought he had enough votes on the floor to win.

Very excited, I went to the House of Representatives on the day of the debate and vote on the city budget. I was in the balcony when Congressman Giaimo's amendment was presented to the congressmen who took a teller vote on the matter. (In a teller vote, congressmen on the floor are given a red or a blue voting square. They pass up two aisles with a box at the end guarded by two "tellers," and they drop the correct color into each box. The tellers count them and report whether or not the amendment has carried.) I looked down during the voting and saw Congressman Boggs standing under the rostrum. He was the House Whip at the time, and he had fifty to seventy-five members grouped around him. They were all watching the voters go up each aisle (and counting). All of a sudden Boggs made his decision in a very dramatic fashion, and he and all of his supporters marched up the "Yes" aisle—and Congressman Giaimo's amendment was adopted.

I was very thrilled and excited, and I rushed into the cloak room to congratulate Congressman Giaimo and to thank Congressman Boggs for the help. Again I was waylaid by General Graham, again he grabbed me by the lapels, again he cried, and again he said, "Hahn you're interfering with my mission which is to build freeways."

The scuffle was interrupted by my administrative assistant (and pal) Bob Walker, who came rushing into the cloak room and said, "Gil, you'd better get back up into the balcony again to see Congressman Andy Jacobs of Indianapolis [known to me as "Crazy Andy"] addressing the House."

"Gentlemen," the Congressman said, "every year I have offered an amendment to the city budget proposing that all cars and drivers in the

Federal Government be eliminated except for the car and driver of the President of the United States, and every year you laugh me down. So this year I am proposing a different amendment, I propose to take away just the car and driver of Gil Hahn, Chairman of the City Council of the District of Columbia. We just voted Hahn $200 million for the subway, let him ride the subway!"

At that time because all of the supporters of Congressman Giaimo and opponents of Congressman Natcher and the Public Works Committee had left the floor, the only ones left were the supporters of Congressman Natcher and the Public Works Committee. As a result, by a voice vote, which appeared to be unanimous, my car and driver vanished. Sometime that fall there was a groundbreaking ceremony to start the subway construction, and I walked to it!

At the time, my salary as council chairman was $15,000, and I received nothing for serving (simultaneously) as chairman and president of the Council of Governments (COG). With all this time taken up by my public duties, I wasn't earning a great deal from my law practice, so the free car (and driver) represented a considerable savings for my family. In fact, the loss of this "perk" had some effect on my decision not to seek a second term.

I thought it important that as an incentive to get commuters to leave their cars at home, the subway fare should be quite low. To offset the loss of revenue, I proposed a regional tax. To this day, I regret the fact that my proposal did not pass.

In any event, the subway *was* built, and it has been and is a great success—and there are no freeways through our beautiful city and no Three Sisters Bridge.

City Council Legacy

Created without much thought during the Lyndon Johnson administration, the D.C. City Council (the first council) was a hodge-podge, a mish-mash, and, for quite a while, simply a mess.

Under the old system, the city had been run by a three-commissioner body whose offices became those of mayor, deputy mayor, and chairman of the city council. Yet they used none of the powers of the old commissioners. For example, while it was spelled out that the chairman acquired the power of the former Engineer Commissioner to say where roads and bridges were to go, nothing was said of the powers of the council itself. Under the first council nothing had happened; they remained little more than a cheering section for the mayor. In fact, during my term, council member Polly

Shackleton—a holdover from the first council—continually asked the deputy mayor what she was allowed to do.

The council I inherited had no organization, no true committee structure, and no legislative agenda or instinct. Finding this deplorable, I set out to change things from top to bottom. The first thing I did was to hold meetings with all the council members and lay out my plans for the kinds of changes that would produce an active, not a passive, council. Unlike the first council, we would legislate by using the police and licensing power given us by the code, *and* we would hold committee hearings—just like any other legislative body—and give the public full access to them as well as to our legislative sessions.

The next thing I examined was the committee structure, which was in shambles. In the past, every little issue had its own ad hoc committee, which produced chaos rather than order. To rectify this, I created an eight-committee structure within which each council member was chairman of a committee, i.e., taxation, health and welfare, and so on. I also introduced my colleagues to the notion of the committee as a whole, of which I was the chairman. I'm pleased to see that the pattern I set up in 1969 is still followed.

Finally, I wanted the city itself to become used to a forceful council, one that would hold hearings and legislate. Realizing I would need television coverage to do this, I persuaded the city's public television station to cover our hearings and legislative sessions. A camera platform was erected, and we were in business. That too survives, in an expanded form. I like to think of these things as my legacy.

The Car Story

One of the things in my career as City Council chairman that loomed all out of proportion was my car and chauffeur, which came complete with radio and mobile phone. I was initiated into the use and customs of these two modes of communication by Montrose, my wonderful driver. The car was mine to use, day and night, and I attached great importance to it, and to Montrose, especially after I lost both.

I'd always felt that my friend Mayor Walter Washington was lording it over me with *his* car and driver and phone, all of which he'd had well before I got mine. So when I did get my car and driver and phone, I immediately called the mayor on his mobile phone in his car. I got him promptly and was about to thank him for the car and driver and phone when he one-upped me by saying, "Excuse me, Gil. My other phone is ringing."

My Three Riots

I got to be fairly immune to riots. Perhaps that was because in my political career I was in at least three of them.

The first took place in 1968, when I was Republican Party chairman for the District of Columbia, just before Richard Nixon's election as president. Candidate Nixon, who was working hard to get some of the African-American vote, pledged that his administration would help African Americans share in the improved economy that he promised for us all. He coined the following as a slogan for African Americans: "Have a piece of the action."

Taking our cue from this, I organized a rally in D.C. in the heart of Black Washington in front of a radio station at 9th and U Streets, Northwest, near Howard University and Griffith Stadium, then the baseball park, to urge African Americans to vote Republican. Sterling Tucker, my future vice chairman of the City Council, lent me a hand in locating the hall and filling the place with prospective voters. We also provided music and beer (the latter being a major mistake).

The meeting started out swimmingly. There was a large and enthusiastic crowd. The speeches went well, and the atmosphere was great. However, at the height of the proceedings, Rufus Catfish Mayfield, a local tough, appeared and jumped onto the stage. He was wearing a kelly green three piece wool suit, and carried a shillelagh. He was accompanied by a gang of roughnecks, including our future "mayor-for-life" Marion Barry, then just a face in the crowd. Mayfield harangued the crowd briefly and then led his gang in throwing beer bottles, which started a melee that broke up the gathering. People were hurt, and we later learned that some of the women were raped. The police came, but could not quell the riot and left! Both Margot and I were lucky not to have been killed. In fact, we might have been, were it not for the timely intercession of Robert (Bob) Campbell, an African American assistant corporation counsel (D.C.'s name for what other jurisdictions call city attorneys) who rescued us. He had heard about the disturbance on his police radio and came to the scene and rescued us. By the time he got there, Margot, Barney Patterson, and I were the only Whites in the crowd. (Bob Campbell was later appointed a judge of Superior Court.)

My second riot took place after I was installed as City Council chairman. I'd held a hearing in the City Council chamber in the District Building (more for show than anything else) on the issue of freeways and subways. I say it was for show because I had already made up my mind not to approve the freeways and to try to get a subway started.

An organization had been created called the Emergency Committee for the Transportation Crises (ECTC). It was headed by a very nice African-American man, Reginald Booker. Marion Barry was among the rabble-rousers in the mob that got up in the chamber and began throwing everything movable at the council members. I got hit by an ashtray (that my staff later engraved for me). The riot broke up the hearing.

I asked Charlie Duncan, the corporation counsel, to order the building guards to come in and restore order. Charlie was Mayor Washington's right hand man, and both he and his boss were pro-freeway and anti-subway. They wanted me to forget about the subways and agree to build the freeways.

"Mr. Chairman," said Duncan, "the Council Chamber is yours. Restore order yourself." He wouldn't provide any help.

I finally had to call Police Chief Jerry Wilson (a wonderful chief who would later become my friend) to come and restore order. As soon as he arrived, he began arresting the worst of the rioters. I went back to my office, and the city reporters gathered round for what they must have thought was going to be a wake. But it didn't turn out that way. In what was obviously an attempt to embarrass me, David Acheson, son of the former Secretary of State Dean Acheson, and an assistant United States attorney dealing with the rioters who had been arrested, called me and tried to get me to charge them with "trespass." I thought that charging someone with trespass in a *public* hearing room was the height of stupidity, and told him so. "Charge them with walking on the grass," I suggested, "fine them five dollars each, and send them home." To my surprise, that's just what he did.

My third major disturbance happened during the antiwar riots of the Vietnam War. There was a huge movement, an "Army," the press would call it, of antiwar demonstrators who came to Washington, camped out on the Mall, and staged a series of marches, many of which resulted in rioting.

As I've reported elsewhere, the administration acted to let the demonstrators protest, have their say, and go home on Sunday, and no one would be hurt. I tried to help by visiting their camps along the Mall at night and by watching the different demonstrations to try and see that nobody got hurt.

The worst riot took place on what was called Mobilization Day, with thousands of protestors rioting on the Capitol grounds. I went up to the Hill with Pete Quesada, who had come to see me on some public business that involved L'Enfant Plaza, which he was then running. General Quesada, a great guy, had headed the Fifth Air Force during World War II. What we beheld was simply an illegal, out-of-hand mob scene. Finally, with the help of the Metropolitan Police, the Capitol Police rounded up hundreds of demonstrators and carted them off to D.C. stadium in buses, where they were processed for trial. (Judge Harold Greene later dismissed all the cases.)

My First Job as a Lawyer, or
Life in the Law Offices of Leon Tobriner

The worst mistake I ever made in my entire legal career was the first one I ever made—accepting a job in the law offices of Leon Tobriner. I did so at the urging of my father, who employed Tobriner to represent the Hahn Shoe Stores, our family business, and I never should have done it. But I had just graduated from Yale law school and passed the bar, and my father, who could be very persuasive, thought it would be good experience. It was not, and the few things I now recall about my time there are either funny or pathetic. The time I spent in that firm did absolutely nothing to advance my career in the law. In fact, the one bit of career advice that Tobriner gave me—to turn down the chance to become Leo Rover's deputy when he was appointed U.S. attorney for the District of Columbia at the beginning of the first Eisenhower administration in 1953—turned out to be completely wrong-headed.

Leon's firm consisted of himself, his son Walter, and a very nice elderly man named Fred Umhau. But then Leon was hardly a spring chicken himself: ninety-two when he hired me, he continued to practice law until his death at age ninety-seven. The firm was so old-fashioned that it not only had rolltop desks, it still had a letter press. A forerunner of carbon paper, the process involved "pressing" letters into bound volumes that were then indexed for future reference, as opposed to carbon copies filed away in file drawers. I can still remember standing at the cigar stand in the lobby of the old Southern Building where our offices were located and listening to the radio, along with all the other loafers, as the Giants' Bobby Thompson hit his famous home run off Ralph Branca of the Dodgers to win the final game of the National League pennant race.

Mr. Tobriner was so old that he had been alive in Washington during the Civil War. He had hunted ducks from a skiff on what is now the Mall, and could recall having seen General Benjamin "Silver Spoon" Butler try cases in the old Federal court house after the Civil War.

Mr. Tobriner did things with a certain style and flair. For example, he always traveled in a chauffeur-driven Packard that he'd acquired at a sale of property confiscated from a convicted rumrunner. My role was to carry his briefcases. In one case, after Leon had finished examining a witness, as we were about to leave, the judge said, "Mr. Tobriner, it's a great pleasure to have you here before us. We don't see you here too often anymore." Tobriner, who heard him as well as I did, said to me in a loud whisper, "What did Judge Holtzoff say?"

I replied, "Mr. Tobriner, Judge Holtzoff says it's a great pleasure to see you here, that he doesn't see you in his court too often anymore."

At that, Tobriner stood and said, "Your honor, it's also a great pleasure to be here before you as this is probably the last case I will ever try in this court." He bowed, as invisible violins played softly in the background and we left to get in the Packard and return to the office.

In the car I said, "Mr. Tobriner, why did you say that to Judge Holtzoff? You know you'll be back in his court again."

"Oh," said Tobriner, "next time I'll think of something else."

Another time a newly appointed judge of the Municipal Court dropped by our office for a visit. He kidded Mr. Tobriner about no longer playing golf, a sport he loved. (Tobriner had played until he was ninety, carefully moving the ball, one short shot after another, down the middle of the fairway at the Woodmont Country Club.)

"Your honor," said Tobriner, "I stopped playing golf after my old friend Louie Levey dropped dead on the golf course. He said, 'It's as good a way to go as any.' But if I dropped dead on the golf course right after Louie, people would say, the old fool, he should have had better sense—and I couldn't stand that."

The Train Story

When I was appointed City Council chairman in 1969, Washington, D.C. was in turmoil. It was the year after the riots following the death of Dr. Martin Luther King, Jr., when whole parts of the city, including several Hahn Shoe Stores, had been burned down. Now there were marches and sit-ins and live-ins to protest the escalation of the war in Vietnam, all of which added to the headaches of running a city that was already divided and disturbed. And if all that wasn't bad enough, Mobilization Day had just been declared, with its planned march on the Pentagon, a surround-and-picket of the Justice Department, and nightly encampments on the Mall.

Walter Washington, then the mayor, and I decided to go to Manhattan and ask our friend John Lindsay, the mayor of New York, for advice on how to run our city during these challenging times. We had intended to fly, but bad weather had the airports socked-in, so we had to take the train, which of course was overcrowded with all the travelers who had planned to fly. After hunting for quite some time, we finally found two seats together and sat down. When we looked around, we discovered we were in a car with a lot of people wearing white jackets with their arms tied across their chests. Pretty soon a man in a blue uniform came along and started counting them.

"One, two, three, four, five, six . . ." He stopped when he got to us. "Who are you?"

Walter spoke up, "This is my colleague Gilbert Hahn, the chairman of the City Council of the District of Columbia, and I'm the Mayor of Washington."

To which the man said, ". . . seven, eight."

Willie Hardy and the Fourth of July

Willie Hardy had a big mouth, yet I grew to love her. Willie Hardy always came to City Council hearings and yelled and screamed insults, imprecations, threats of riots, and demands that we cure all the ills of the Black community.

This took some getting used to, but in the end I made an important discovery: Willie Hardy didn't mean any of this personally, and she would have been offended if I had taken it personally. Of course one can be mistaken about these things. Some Black activists did mean their slurs and insults personally, but, on the whole, I found that you could—and should— get used to it. And, once you did, it made politics in the melting pot of the District of Columbia livable, and it gave you a proper perspective of what was going on. I figured out that if you couldn't accept politics on these terms you were probably in the wrong business in the first place. I mention Willie Hardy and her big mouth because of the Fourth of July.

In 1969, the Fourth of July had been a municipal disaster. The program had gone all wrong. Looting, rioting, assault, and rape had taken place indiscriminately on the Monument grounds where the ceremonies were held. People were robbed, people were hurt, and thousands and thousands of patriots who normally attended the Fourth of July celebration, and looked forward to it with their children, vowed never to come again.

So, as the time for planning the Fourth of July 1970 approached, the normal organizers of the Fourth of July—the United States Park Service and the city government as well as the Washington Board of Trade—decided among themselves that in 1970 the Fourth of July would be canceled.

Unhappily, nobody seemed too excited about this development. The situation in the city was such that with a riot and demonstration seemingly every weekend, the exhausted authorities, the several police forces, and the Park Service quite naturally decided, "Who needs this?"

To my surprise, one fine morning, Willie Hardy marched into my office, and said, "Mr. Chairman, what's this I hear about not having the Fourth of July this year?" I thought to myself, *What's with Willie Hardy and the Fourth of July? It is not Martin Luther King's birthday or some such ceremony.* But I held my tongue.

"Mr. Chairman, what's the matter with you anyhow? You should be ashamed of yourself. How can we not celebrate Independence Day?"

"Willie, we don't need any more riots on the Monument grounds. You remember what happened last year. We have a riot and a demonstration every weekend in this city. I don't think the people who run the Fourth of July need another riot with raping, robberies and injuries. And, anyhow, nobody will come to it."

"Mr. Chairman, I tell you, it's disgraceful, and you of all people ought to be ashamed of yourself. You organize the Fourth of July, and there won't be any rioting, raping, or disturbances."

"Come on, Willie."

"Mr. Chairman, you get the Fourth of July going and trust me. There won't be a thing take place on the Monument grounds.

What I did next was, of course, totally irresponsible.

I got together with the Board of Trade, the Park Service, and Chief Wilson, and I persuaded them to have the Fourth of July. "Trust me," I said, "there won't be a single wrong thing take place on the Monument grounds."

The Park Service, the Board of Trade, and Chief Wilson grudgingly agreed to hold the Fourth of July—and they generously provided the necessary fireworks, music, and police support. In return, I had agreed to publicize the Fourth of July and "guarantee" a safe and sane Fourth at the Monument grounds.

The Fourth of July ceremonies were duly announced. I gathered up Margot and our three very small children and nervously took my place in the front-row seats for the ceremony. I opened the proceedings with a nondescript welcome, which was duly booed and applauded. The band played. The fireworks were magnificent. Everybody had a good time. Nobody that I knew of got robbed, raped, or hurt.

I loved it that Willie Hardy had shamed me into rescuing the Fourth of July. But it was twenty-two years before I dared tell anybody that Willie Hardy and her big mouth had "guaranteed" a safe and sane Fourth of July.

The President of the United States Wants You to Raise the Real Estate Tax Tomorrow

In his second year as mayor, Walter Washington, wanting to fatten the District's coffers by several million dollars, proposed raising the D.C. real estate tax fifteen cents per hundred dollars as part of the 1971 budget. He did not, however, want to take the blame for such a move; he wanted his good friend Gil Hahn to be the fall guy. The problem was that a central part of my most important programs as head of the City Council was *not* to raise the real estate tax on homes in the District of Columbia. Washington, at the time, was a home-owning community. The average homeowner, Black or White, felt the impact of real estate taxes more severely than other citizens. One important reason for this was that taxpayers who itemized their deductions for federal taxes could deduct real estate taxes. The ordinary wage-earner could not. Consequently a raise in the real estate tax fell directly upon most of my constituents' pockets.

As the power to raise real estate taxes fell within the province of the City Council, the mayor very shrewdly calculated that the blame for the tax increase would fall on the City Council and not on himself. As a result, I laid a plan before my fellow council members to cut from the mayor's budget that amount of money that would have been raised by the real estate tax increase. (I'd had the council study the issue, and we'd determined that we could legitimately cut enough fat from the mayor's budget to avoid having to raise the tax.) I persuaded my colleagues on the council to go along with my proposed changes. We then adopted a proposal not to raise real estate taxes and to cut the budget.

Once this budget proposal had been returned to the mayor, he was furious. He sent messages to my colleagues that, for the most part, cowed them all. What's more, he used his considerable influence at the White House in an attempt to persuade me to change my mind. The reason Walter had that amount of influence was an interesting one. This is how it came about: when President Nixon was all set to introduce his cabinet, he discovered he had no Black person present. At the last moment, he persuaded Walter, whom he was reappointing as mayor, to appear on television with his cabinet nominees to show the nation and the world that he, Richard Nixon, was sensitive to Black Americans. The high price that Walter extracted for agreeing to do this shrewdly included the patronage in the District of Columbia and a sympathetic ear to whatever Walter wanted within the same province.

We were getting ready for a council meeting the following day to vote on my motion to keep real estate taxes as they were. I went to bed that night anticipating an unexciting tomorrow. About 2 a.m., however, the phone rang, waking both Margot and me. I picked up the phone and an operator came on and said, "Mr. Hahn the White House calling." Then, as today, I expect those words wake anyone up thoroughly and concentrate the mind.

Richard Nathan, who had succeeded Bud Krogh as a staffer in charge of District of Columbia affairs, came on the phone with no preamble and stated, "Hahn [not "Gil" or "Mr. Hahn"], the president of the United States wants you to raise the real estate taxes tomorrow morning by 15 cents." It struck me immediately that Walter Washington had been throwing his weight around.

Still feeling playful I responded, "The president of the United States doesn't give a shit what the real estate tax is in the District of Columbia. He pays people like me to worry about things like this. Dick, you are butting into a fight between the mayor and me. Butt out of it, and let us settle the matter."

"You couldn't be more mistaken," said Nathan. "The president does want you to raise real estate taxes tomorrow morning, and if you don't we'll get another boy to be chairman of the City Council." I said, "Goodnight Dick, and I really mean goodnight." With that, I went back to bed.

The next morning there was pure terror at the City Council. Looking pale and nervous, Sterling Tucker said, "Mr. Chairman we better not go through with this plan of yours. I've gotten telephone calls from the White House." I said, "Sterling we're not going to raise real estate taxes this morning, so forget about it. In any case, there is nothing to worry about," I said, not at all convinced myself.

To my immense relief, after some "coaxing" on my part, the rest of the council stood firm in their support of me, and we acted on real estate taxes by not raising them. The only one to speak and vote against it was Sterling himself.

Two results followed. One was long lasting, that is, real estate taxes on private homes and apartment houses in the District of Columbia have not been raised from that day to this. The other result was that subsequently elected politicians in the mayor's office or on the City Council have honored "Hahn's rule." You don't raise real estate taxes in the District of Columbia.

Actually there was one other result. Still sore about the pressure that Mr. Nathan had put on me, I contacted some friends of my own at the White House and communicated my displeasure over his heavy-handedness. To my amazement, they got rid of him! They sent him off to become assistant secretary someplace. Not too long ago, he was appointed to an important deanship at Princeton's Woodrow Wilson School of Public and International Affairs, my alma mater!

*   *   *   *   *

The tax story has an addendum. After all the dust had settled, for some reason I can no longer recall, I began to be suspicious about Ken Back, the man in charge of the real estate assessments for the District. A very able and sophisticated man, probably the most able and sophisticated we'd ever had in that job, Back happened to be sly, or so I had begun to think. One day when we had him before the council on some routine matter, I put a question to him. "Mr. Back," I said, "tell me how you assess real estate in the District of Columbia."

He replied that he reduced the market value, or "level of assessment," figure by 55%, and then based the tax on the lower amount.

"You are not," I inquired, "trying to circumvent the Council's action in blocking the tax increase by fiddling with the level of assessment and raising it to 60 or 65%, are you?"

"Oh no," he promised, and then, after I had dragged it out of him, he also promised he would never do so in the future either.

In 1972, by which time I had returned to private practice, one of my former assistants on the council, a dedicated public servant who was also a political activist, came to see me. He said there was something "funny" going on with the real estate taxes. He eventually brought into my office a small group of taxpayers who all thought they had the same assessed valuation, but their taxes had all gone up either 5 or 10%. The result of their coming to me was what became known as the Green case (*Green v. The District of Columbia*). We sued on the basis that the city had illegally raised the taxes by 5 or 10% by an unauthorized hike in the assessment levels. At trial, we proved that the District had done just what Mr. Back had promised me he would not do—the city had raised some (but not all) taxes by 5% by raising the level of assessment, and the amount they recovered was exactly what had been lost when I blocked the tax increase. What a coincidence!

The judge, whose decision was later upheld by the Court of Appeals, set aside the increases and ordered refunds for thousands of District taxpayers. It should come as no surprise that for quite a while I was a very popular fellow in the city.

Hospitals and Meg Greenfield

A few years before I became City Council chairman, I went on the Board of the Washington Hospital Center. In 1967, I became president of the Board.

It was a fact of life in D.C. that the Washington Hospital Center was looked down upon by the other hospitals. It had been created during World War II by combining Emergency, Episcopal, and Garfield—three small, old hospitals. The good news was that the Hospital Center had been given a large part of the land of the Old Soldiers Home near the Veterans' Administration Hospital, but the bad news was this was a part of town where noone from Northwest Washington wanted to come if they didn't have to.

With the guidance of the then-administrator Dick Loughery, and the support of the doctors on the board, plus most of the lay members, we turned it into an excellent and very successful hospital. In fact, by the 1990s it was the only successful hospital in the city, most of the others having fallen on hard times.

Here are just a few of the things that we did. We advertised. We started an endowment fund. We built the basis for a heart complex that became the city's best. We gave the "lakefront" (i.e., the land facing the McMillan Reservoir) to Children's Hospital for $1.00 to get them to come there and build a new hospital complex and to make the place a "campus." We saved the School of Nursing. We created a research facility and built the best luxury suites (to this day) in the country.

After I left the board to become the City Council chairman in 1969, the hospital progressed and prospered as part of the Medlantic Medical complex.

Not long after serving my term as council chairman, I was appointed chairman of the new board of the city's public hospital, D.C. General. In the 1970s, D.C. General had lost its accreditation and was losing a lot of money. With the help of Robert Johnson, an excellent administrator I found there, we put that hospital back on its feet. Our accreditation got restored—after a lot of hard work. More than that, we found that the hospital was making no effort to collect third-party payments. When we began collecting them, we raised $5 million the first year, which was increased by another $5 million each year thereafter. By the fifth year, we reached a plateau and could not further increase these recoveries.

$5 million every year about matched the yearly increase in the cost of operating the hospital, so I went to the mayor (at this point Marion Barry) for the extra money—about $5 million for that year's rise in costs.

He said he didn't want to give it to the hospital.

I said if he wanted to save the money so badly, his best move was to shut down the hospital and pay the private hospitals to care for the non-covered patients. No, he said, cut costs. I replied that would result in the loss of all that we had achieved and worked for so far.

And so it proved. After my resignation, the hospital lost its accreditation and, at my last reading in 1995, was costing the city in the neighborhood of $100 million a year to operate. I had asked to be relieved and advised Bob Johnson to leave as well. He did and took another job at a fine hospital in St. Louis. A good man, he too predicted what was going to happen.

However, before the fall, when we achieved our success of restoring accreditation, the *Washington Post* published a wonderful editorial entitled "The Hospital That Got Well," praising what we had accomplished.

I called my friend Meg Greenfield (now alas deceased) to thank her.

"Gil," she said, "don't get carried away. If I was in a car accident and woke up in the ambulance, and asked 'Where are you taking me?' and they said, 'D.C. General,' I would have said, 'Don't bother, take me straight to Gawlers [a famous funeral home in Washington].'"

*   *   *   *   *

All of that happened in the 1970s. For the next couple of decades I continued to have a rooting interest in D.C. General. Then, in about 1998 or 1999, in the midst of the worst budget crisis under Mayor Marion Barry, my friend Sterling Tucker and I were asked by the *Washington Post* to write about the city's various problems.

In my articles (unlike Sterling's), the focus was on how to help people. I chose to discuss the ways in which it might be possible to save the city from waste and corruption, and I used D.C. General Hospital as a prime example.

I said that if we were to close the wasteful facility and pay private hospitals to care for the city's free patients, even if we had to pay the private hospitals' full rates, it would mean a $50 million savings per year.

In response, the hospital's public relations man wrote the *Post* and stated, publicly, that the hospital was making a profit. I challenged that by asking him to produce the annual statement, and he did so. I went through it and was able to show him that even if we used *his* accounting, the hospital was in fact losing almost $100 million a year.

Not long after that, Tony Williams, the newly elected mayor, created a D.C. Health Commission to take up D.C. health problems, with an emphasis on health care for the needy, noninsured patients, and the possible creation of many primary care facilities. The mayor appointed me to the commission. I was assigned to the committee charged with looking into increasing the primary care facilities. The committee's chairman, an energetic public health doctor, wanted to create new primary care facilities. When he was told there was no money for that purpose, I piped up and said, "I know how to free up $50 million—close D.C. General."

The doctor, his committee staff, and all the rest of the commission members were aghast at this suggestion and openly hostile to it. You couldn't close D.C. General. It was a sacred cow. They were against the idea.

D.C. General itself entered the fray by stating, once again, that it had made a profit the previous year. Once again, I asked to see the statement and began an investigation. The statement turned out to be quite a piece of work. Instead of making a profit, D.C. General owed the city $60 million over and above the city's regular annual subsidy, but the city had forgiven the debt. However, on its books, the hospital had treated the debt forgiveness as "income." So, obviously the city was losing more than $100 million a year over and above the subsidy.

I investigated and found a letter from the accountant that stated the CEO of the hospital, Ken Fairman, a Barry appointee and clone, had directed the hospital's CPA to treat the item as income. The so-called profit was a fraud. Further investigation showed that Fairman had been hiring his friends as (nonworking) staff members of existing city posts and giving favored friends contracts to supply the hospital, but without putting the contracts up for bidding by anyone else.

After I'd released my report, Margot told me she feared employees of D.C. General would picket me and would make angry phone calls. But just the opposite happened. They called with congratulations and gave me chapter-and-verse on even more abuses, and said, "Go to it, Gil. It's a disgrace."

Finally, the new mayor stepped in and arranged for an independent investigating firm to examine the hospital. Its report was even less favorable than mine. In addition to the ghost hires and the false accounting, the firm documented that D.C. General was inflating the number of patients they were treating and concluded its report by recommending the hospital be closed.

As it turned out, Alice Rivlin and the D.C. Control Board had already done a study that had come to the same conclusion, but the report had been suppressed. Within a few months, the mayor closed D.C. General and set up a new—and successful—system for treating free cases.

His critics on the City Council and some members of the clergy, acting for political gain, have been critical of this decision, but from where I sit, it looks like Mayor Williams will be the winner in the end.

Mayor Anthony Williams

I have always cared a lot about the city of Washington. That was one reason why I used the symbol "Give A Damn" when I was City Council chairman.

In Mayor Anthony (Tony) Williams, Washington, D.C., has found another citizen who gives a damn about the city. I like him fine, and he is mayor as we speak.

Because of him, I committed a brief heresy and strayed, momentarily, from my political affiliation, and career, as a Republican.

When Tony announced he would run for mayor in the Democratic primary, I did something I thought I would never do—I became a Democrat—for thirty days.

This is briefly how it happened.

After Walter Washington's first elected term as mayor, a crass and calculating rabble-rouser named Marion Barry captured the Democratic nomination and got elected mayor for two terms, and then was sent to jail. (During that time, an equally inept clone named Mrs. Kelly was elected in his place; following his lead, she hurt the city as much as he had.) After his release, Barry ran for yet another term, and was elected once again.

Barry's outrageous method of operation was to stuff the city's job rolls with his incompetent friends. He cared nothing for the way the city was to take care of its duties and constantly ran up deficits. Among other things, he appointed a man named Ken Fairman to run D.C. General Hospital and the Public Health Service. Fairman carried out his duties as a carbon copy of his patron, Marion "Mayor-for-life" Barry. Finally, things got so out of hand that the Congress created a Control Board (sort of like trustees in bankruptcy for the city) to take financial control of the city away from Barry and try to restore order, and at least a semblance of good government, to the city.

One of the first things the Control Board made Barry do was hire a financial officer to run the city's books and keep financial controls. Barry could hire this person, but he had no power to fire him. The man he chose was Tony Williams, a financial officer at the Department of Agriculture.

Tony had a degree from Harvard and two degrees from Yale. The city and I were duly impressed, and we paid attention to him.

It didn't take long for friction to develop between Barry and Williams. Soon the papers were filled with stories about Tony Williams threatening to quit because he and Barry, two oh-so-different men, disagreed about this, that, and the other—naturally.

Each time another "I threaten to quit" letter was run in the local papers, I would take notice of them and dash off a letter to Tony urging him *not* to quit. We didn't know each other, and in fact had never even met, but to me he looked like someone the citizens ought to rally behind and encourage to stay the course.

I doubt if he ever paid any attention to my letters, but in fact he did not quit. Not only that, but as the next election period loomed, a group of movers and shakers in the Democratic Party who were tired of Marion Barry organized, raised money, and backed Williams as the Democratic candidate.

Then, as now, nomination on the Democratic ticket meant certain election in Washington.

Even though I was a former Republican Party chairman in the city, I wanted this man to become our mayor. So I took myself to the election board, switched parties, and offered my services to the primary election campaign of Tony Williams. Tony and his backers were so pleased they carried me around from meeting to meeting as a symbol (or lucky charm).

At the fair number of rallies I attended on behalf of Williams, I was always introduced as the former Republican Party chairman and former City Council head, which was always good for cheers and a hearty round of applause.

I had some small guilt feelings about Williams' Republican opponent, Carol Schwartz, who had run against Marion Barry in the previous election and made a credible showing. Not only is Carol a friend, but her husband had worked for me as general counsel for the City Council while I was chairman. Carol remains a good City Council member, but I felt the city had been abused for so long by Barry and Kelly that we deserved Williams, whom I believed could and would do wonderful things for Washington.

When thirty days had passed, I took myself back to the election board and resumed my Republican identity, but having cast in the meantime my Democratic vote in the Democratic primary for Williams and helped raise Republican money for his cause.

In the general election, I was put forward as head of "Republicans for Williams," but Tony's brain trust decreed that such a group was not needed, as Tony would win easily, and they were right.

Tony still has a long way to go to undo all the harm caused by Marion Barry—like hiring ex-felons to be on the police force. If that weren't bad enough, Williams has discovered that the civil service system makes it very difficult to weed out all the unqualified Barry appointees as quickly as he would like.

Nonetheless, Tony has made great progress, and his election was no mistake. To make just one point of proof, during the Barry/Kelly era, the city's bonds were rated as junk bonds; once Tony Williams was elected, they became investment-grade overnight.

Tony appointed me to his Health Commission, and the story of that work and the "disposition" of D.C. General Hospital appears elsewhere in this notebook.

Margot and I have become good friends with Tony and his wife, Diane, who have spent several weekends with us at Meetinghouse Cove for several years.

As this is written, Tony has been excellent in dealing with city problems following the terrorist raid on the Pentagon and the anthrax problem.

We are proud of him.

* * * * *

Now that Tony is solidly in office, the movers and shakers of the Democratic Party are looking ahead to the next election, even if it is two and a half years away. A "Committee to Re-Elect Tony Williams" has been formed. I am a member. And a monster fundraiser was held during the closing days of the Clinton administration.

I was not the only Republican involved in the event, which raised over $700,000. Bob Dole was co-chairman, and other Republican notables attended. The big event took place at the home of Beth Dezoritz (of The Great Pardon fame).

I'd never met President Clinton, but he appeared for Tony's big fund raiser and gave the principal speech. Margot and I watched as he came into the room. Bigger than life, he made eye contact with everyone in the room. He made a beeline for Margot—and shook hands with me, too. Never, since seeing Ike at the 1952 convention in Chicago, had I seen another person with such genuine "animal magnetism." I can now understand how the man did it. Spectacular.

Chapter 2

ಎಂಡಿ

Politics, Politicians, and . . .

Young Republicans for Vandenberg

This story is about my first experience in politics. It involves Arthur Vandenberg and the 1948 Republican Convention, which was held in Philadelphia.

In 1948, I was at Yale Law School, and with very few exceptions my classmates and I had been in the war. You might say that after the war was over, we began to learn the law. The 1948 convention, which was to be held for the Republican Party (and I guess also for the Democrats that year) in Philadelphia, was to pick a nominee to oppose Harry Truman, who was running for his second term as president. Governor Dewey had run against Franklin Roosevelt in 1944 and lost in a fairly close race, but he had a lot of opposition in the Republican Party. In my opinion, the Republican Party, at that time centered in the northeastern and midwestern states and California, probably had the most attractive group of candidates. Among others there was Senator Taft of Ohio, Senator Bricker of Ohio, Governor Warren of California, Senator Vandenberg, and many other interesting fiscally conservative and socially liberal politicians; of course, this description also included both Dewey and Taft. Dewey had run well against Roosevelt during the war, but a number of candidates tried to take the play away from him.

At that time, to those of us at Yale Law School of the liberal Republican persuasion, the most attractive candidate was Senator Vandenberg. Senator Vandenberg represented a cooperation in foreign policy with the existing Democratic administration, and at the time he was the Republican Party's poster boy.

A group of us formed an ad hoc organization called Young Republicans for Vandenberg, and I became its chairman. It included my good friends John Lindsay and Powell Pierpoint. A group of about twenty of us put together a list of what we had done in the war and of all the medals we had won. We sent this letter to Vandenberg, telling him that we wanted to support him as our candidate for president of the United States. After a while, we got a letter back from him in which he said (essentially) the following: "Gentlemen, I am not a candidate for President and I don't want to be President. If I wanted to put together an organization to help me become President, you are the last group of people I would pick." Then he said, "On the other hand, if we ever have a war again . . ."

Undaunted, Powell and I went to Philadelphia where the convention was held. In those days, you didn't need a ticket or anything else to get onto the convention floor. You just walked in, which we did, and we spent two or three days having a rather good time talking to the different delegates and the heads of the different state organizations. Dewey got the nomination and went on to his second defeat, but the best of the weekend was still to come.

We were invited to meet Claire Boothe Luce, who was the actual chairman of the draft-Vandenberg organization. (While I was in law school at Yale, I had occasionally been invited to parties at the Luce home where I found her to be a captivating lady. She always had gathered all the men at the party around her. Every once in a while, though, Mr. Luce would come into the room and divide the party up again.) She received us in her hotel suite in the Belleview Stratford, reclining on a chaise lounge and wearing a negligee (!), and thanked us for trying to help Vandenberg. I thought to myself, *if this is what politics is like, this is for me!* (Sadly, I have to report that this was the high point; it has been downhill ever since.)

General Eisenhower, the Nomination in 1952, and the Fair Play Amendment

In 1952, I was beginning both my law practice in the District of Columbia and my career as an amateur politician in the Young Republican Club, along with fellow attorney Carl Shipley. In order to generate public interest in our organization, Carl and I had a Sunday radio program on WGMS, the Good Music Station, called "View Point: The Washington Forum of the Air." We advertised ourselves as Gilbert Hahn, Jr. and Carl L. Shipley, "prominent Washington attorneys" (though we were hardly that at the time), and for some months our guests were local and national political figures whom we interviewed on various public topics. To our surprise, we did quite well. In fact, we regularly drew higher ratings than the famous program from Chicago, "Meet the Press," which went on at the same time.

For a while, our sponsor was a local furniture store. We kept that client until the day we inadvertently interviewed the chairman of the local board of trade, who was also in the furniture business. Our sponsor promptly fired us.

Back in those days, the Republican Party of the District of Columbia was typical of all Republican organizations outside of the north and west, meaning it was small enough to hold its meetings in a closet or telephone booth. The heads of the local party were Joe McGaraghy, my particular friend and later my patron, and Jimmy Wilkes, Joe's law partner. The national committeeman was a Mr. Ed Colladay, a local lawyer who was, in fact, the senior national committeeman. Ours was typical of Republican organizations in the normally Democratic South, meaning it existed only to raise money for national elections (and to hope that during a Republican administration its members might get some kind of political preference, especially in the case of lawyers for judgeships).

The year 1952, however, was of special interest because even from a long way off it looked like the Republicans were going to gain the presidency that year, no matter who ran as the candidate. In the end, there were only two principal candidates. One was the star of the conservative wing of the party, Robert A. Taft of Ohio, a scion of the famous Taft family, and the other was noncandidate General Dwight D. Eisenhower, hero of World War II. In the past, everything that the D.C. Republican Party had ever done was always done in secret. Under the cover of closed meetings, all business was conducted by the members of the state committee, who'd been appointed by the chairman, and selected by the party chairman, committeeman, committeewoman, finance chairman, and the delegates, and six alternates were usually chosen from among the party faithful and/or the substantial party givers, as for example, Mr. and Mrs. Willard Marriott. Because of the critical importance of the nomination in 1952—and the near certainty that whoever got the nomination would win—the contest was serious and severe. Thus even in the typically moribund Southern part of the Republican Party, unusual activity took place.

In those days, there was no Republican Party as such south of the Mason-Dixon line. In fact, frequently more than one delegation showed up at the National Convention, so there was often a lot of work for the credentials committee in determining which delegation to seat. In the District of Columbia, the interest was running high, because the *Washington Post* and the *Washington Evening Star*, the two main local papers at the time, were pushing for Dwight Eisenhower, and most of the party stalwarts were determined to give the nomination to Bob Taft.

Let me just say in passing that the Republican Party of that era was a far cry from the Republican Party of today. To call the 1952 Republican Party a conservative party was really a misnomer. The conservative party in national politics was the Southern wing of the Democratic Party, which typically overshadowed the whole Democratic Party, whose liberal element was made up of labor unions in the north, the big city machines like Tammany Hall in New York City, and the various liberal elite. In terms of today's politics, those standout Republicans of 1952 would have been considered "raving liberals."

Among those who fit that description were Earl Warren, Arthur Vandenburg, and Senator Bricker of Ohio, as well as Governor Dewey of New York, and various Republican stalwarts of New England and the upper Midwest. Nevertheless, the conservative wing of the Republican Party, which was dead set on getting Bob Taft the nomination for president, had total control of the Republican National Committee and appointed all the committees and committee chairmen, as well as the chairman of the convention, which was set to take place at the stockyards in Chicago. Because of all of this competition and scrambling for delegates, much more interest than usual was focused on the choice of delegates to the convention from the District of Columbia. As a result of that, the party determined to change its usual habits and to put up for election the members of the D.C. Republican committee by vote in open caucuses in about thirty to fifty places around the city. The idea was that anyone who came in and registered and said he or she was a member of the Republican Party of the District of Columbia would then be allowed to vote.

The biggest contest took place at the caucus that was set for the Wardman Park Hotel. Joe McGaraghy, my friend and patron who was running for a member of the state committee, was opposed by Bob McLaughlin, who later became president of the Board of Commissioners of the District of Columbia. The turnout was enormous—for a Republican caucus vote in the District of Columbia. I had done a lot of work for McGaraghy in the District and in the different caucuses in the city, all of which, though highly contested, were figured to be won by the Taft supporters.

I went door-to-door for Joe in Ward 3, and in what was then the District of Columbia's biggest precinct contest, Joe, with my aid, beat the Eisenhower opponent. Indeed, the Taft candidates for the "State" Committee won across the board. With the State Committee committed to Taft, the delegates and alternates selected were all Taft supporters—except for me. I wanted Dwight Eisenhower, my old commander-in-chief, to run and win.

When the delegates met, it was agreed that our six votes would be cast as unanimous. As I had no choice, I agreed, along with the others (the six actual delegates and the six alternates). But then I spoke up. "Be practical. The Republican Party in the District is small. We have no independent clout. It is in the local party's interest to have voted for the winner. You think Taft will win, I think Ike will win. Will you agree to cast our six votes for Ike if it looks like he will win?" To their credit, they all agreed.

We all descended on Chicago in the heat of summer. Margot went with me, and we stayed with her uncle and aunt. The convention was held in the stockyards, a truly awful place with dirt floors because of its more usual activities. Still, it turned out to be a *very* exciting week. My friend Carl Shipley (later the party secretary and later still its chairman) and I circulated among our (generally younger) contemporaries in the different State delegations, who were, like us, active in the National Young Republicans. (For the record, I had managed Carl Shipley's unsuccessful campaign for National Young Republican president. We had lost, but we had given them a scare, so we were well-known by, and friends with, all these young tigers who were rising in their own state's regular Republican Party. Because of this, Carl and I, passing back and forth among the delegations, probably had the best count of the delegates votes, and as a result, we concluded that it would be close but Ike would win.)

I came back to our delegation and reported what I had found. I reminded them of our agreement to vote for the winner. Among the people I talked to next was Cliff Roberts, an experienced Pol from Kansas City, who was one of Ike's confidential backers. "It's close," he said. "Can we get even a couple of votes from your delegation?" In my enthusiasm I told him I hoped to get them all, and I went to sleep that night dreaming of being made *at least* secretary of state in the new administration.

The real action began the next day. The Taft forces, who had complete control of the convention, had put Taft supporters in control of all the important committees, and the atmosphere of the convention was tense. When it began to appear that Ike might win, the Taft people were outraged. They felt Taft was entitled, and discouraged support of Ike. (Margot, who was pregnant with our first child, sat with the other wives in the balcony. Because I was for Ike, Margot worried that the Taft wives might throw her out of the balcony—or *over* it.)

Each side was allowed a set of speakers who would alternately address the highly charged delegate hall and television audience. The final speaker was Senator Everett Dirksen of Illinois. A famously old-fashioned and old-school orator, he spoke in rounded tones and colorful turns of phrase. His nearest likeness was Maryland's governor, Theodore Roosevelt McKelden, no slouch himself, who was to be Ike's nominating speaker.

As Dirksen strode to the podium to speak, the audience and the delegates roared in anticipation, as if for a great climax. This is how I remember it to this day: Dirksen began, "As a Republican faithful, I went to Old Orchard Beach, Maine, to address the local Republican Party faithful, on the beach. As I arose to speak, there was a great roar, and I was alarmed. And I showed my alarm, and they said to me, Congressman, don't be alarmed, it's only the tide rolling in."

As everyone in the place understood, he was referring to the strong probability that Taft would be beaten and that the "tide" of delegate votes would be to amend the credential committee's report in Ike's favor.

Then, he pointed to Dewey, who was sitting in the front row with the huge New York delegation with Brownell, whom all knew had managed to place the amendment on the floor to seat the Ike delegations.

And Dirksen roared, "You led us down the path to defeat twice before." The place broke out in an uproar, and nothing more got heard after that. In the voting that followed, Ike's delegates were seated, and with help from Harold Stassen, Ike later won, and the rest was history.

I should explain that at this time the most important committee was the Credentials Committee. 1952 was the end of the era of the Solid South; the two-party system in the South wouldn't start until the Goldwater campaign of 1964. Because of the complete political dominance by the Democrats in the South, the various Republican parties in the southern states were not parties at all, but a collection of a few people (a lot of lawyers) who met, as I said earlier, in telephone booths and called themselves the Republican Party of, say, South Carolina. Often more than one group claimed to represent a single southern state, sometimes as many as three or four. They would appear at the convention with (disputed) claims to be the party of, say, South Carolina.

The Credentials Committee had the initial job of sorting out these claims and issuing a report that proposed to the convention which delegation should be seated. This year two delegations presented themselves from Texas and Louisiana: one set was for Taft and the other for Eisenhower. Naturally, the Taft-controlled Credentials Committee issued its report and in each case proposed to seat the Taft delegation. In a normal convention, that would have been that. Not this time.

Herbert (Herb) Brownell, who had managed the Dewey campaign in 1948, and before, had a plan. Dewey led the huge New York delegation, which was pledged to Ike, and Brownell was his ally. When the Credentials Committed report was presented to the convention, Brownell rose to offer an amendment to the report asking to seat the Eisenhower delegates. He called it the "Fair Play" amendment. A debate was set, and several hours of debate followed. But Brownell had persuaded the undecided votes.

The amendment was adopted, seating the Eisenhower delegates from Texas and Louisiana. This was enough to keep Taft from winning—but not quite enough to give Ike the majority.

Between the two sessions (the nominations and voting would come next), Ike arrived in Chicago and was interviewed by the press on television.

"General," a reporter asked, "isn't it setting a precedent for a candidate to come to the convention?"

"Well, yes," said Ike. "I guess this is a precedent. I'm not much for precedents, but then neither am I against them much."

That night our delegation was invited to meet Ike. All during the war I had, of course, never seen Ike, up close or even from afar, but in his presence I was overwhelmed. I had never before been in the presence of someone with such what I'll call animal magnetism. I left more determined than ever to do my level best to help him win.

After a stem-winding nominating speech for Ike by Theodore McKelden, the Republican governor of Maryland, the convention began to vote for the presidential nomination. The margin was razor-thin. All the votes were cast for Taft or Eisenhower, neither achieving a majority (except in Minnesota, which voted for its favorite son, Harold Stassen). I was keeping a tally in the back, and when the voting got to Wyoming, it became clear to me that Ike could win.

We voted next, and then Puerto Rico with its three votes, to be followed by Hawaii and Alaska with six votes each. (Puerto Rico caused a furor by asking the convention secretary to poll the delegation.) Alaska was pledged to give Ike all its votes, which would leave Ike three votes short of a majority, which meant that the District's six votes for Ike would make him the candidate for, and then *the*, president.

I was sitting in the back with the alternates and with Joe McGaraghy's partner Jimmie Wilkes and our national committeeman Ed Colladay, both of whom were devoted to Taft. They looked at each other across me, and one of them said, "Gil is right. Ike is going to win. Let's go tell Joe to switch our vote to Ike. We should honor our promise to Gil to cast our six votes for Ike if he's going to win."

At that very moment, Joe McGaraghy, the delegation's chairman, was being called by the convention chairman to announce the District vote. McGaraghy was trying to pass, but he was so nervous that instead of handing over the mike he was holding on to it like grim death.

Martin Agronsky, the television pioneer, who was covering the convention live from the floor, said, coast-to-coast, "The District can't even pass properly." Just then, Jimmie Wilkes and I fought our way through a wall of people in the aisle to reach McGaraghy. As the younger, I had Jimmie by the hand and was using my football training to knock the crowd apart so that Jimmie and I could get to McGaraghy.

When we made it, Jimmie said to his partner, "Joe, Gil is right. We should honor our promise to him to cast our vote for Ike if he looks to win." But the party secretary, George Hart, objected, saying, "Our votes won't put Ike over the top."

I said, "George, Alaska and our vote will give Ike a majority."

Joe McGaraghy then said, "None of that is important. Taft won our votes and even if and when Ike is elected, we will still have Taft in Washington. We should vote for Taft and then switch to Ike on the next round."

"Joe," I said, "I know you want a judgeship on the Court of Appeals. If you do this you won't get appointed." Nonetheless, he cast the votes for Taft. However, before the second vote, Harold Stassen switched his votes to Ike, and it was all over. The District never got to switch its vote. (Taft did not return to the Senate for very long. He soon died of cancer, which I always supposed was brought on by a broken heart.)

Joe McGaraghy, who became Inaugural Committee chairman, was later appointed a District Court judge. George Hart also got a District Court judgeship. Carl Shipley became D.C. party chairman. Leo Rover, the new district attorney, offered me the job of first assistant D.A. I said no, but I've often wondered how that would have changed my life and career had I accepted.

The Inaugural Medal

During the preparations for the inauguration of Dwight Eisenhower in 1952, I was appointed as chairman of the Inaugural Medal Committee by the local Republican chairman, Joe McGaraghy. This was a minor appointment. The major committees then were "Parade" and "Inaugural Ball."

In all the past inaugurations, the U.S. Mint had made the Inaugural Medal, which never appeared until long after the inauguration and thus was purchased by only a few collectors. In 1952, however, the word came down from the general himself that he wanted his inauguration to symbolize private enterprise. So, I arranged with the Medallic Arts Company, a small but highly respected firm, to produce the medal instead of the Mint.

Quite a while before the inauguration, a well-respected sculptor named Hancock did a bust of the general, and this was used to make the front of the medal. I organized as much publicity as I could, by virtue of ads purchased by the companies that provided the gold, silver, and bronze for the three types of medals. We made two gold medals, one each for President Eisenhower and Vice President Nixon. The silver were a limited number at a higher price, with each silver medal stamped with a number.

The gold medals were duly presented by Chairman McGaraghy, and I arranged for volunteer ladies to set up card tables in all the hotels in the city to take orders for the sale of the silver and bronze replicas. The whole thing was so successful that the income from the sale almost matched the totals for the parade and the balls.

For the second inauguration of Eisenhower and Nixon, I was again appointed as medal chairman, and this time the sale of the medals was the highest income-earner for the entire inauguration. In all the successive inaugurations, the sale of medals has been even larger and more profitable.

Later, I did some research on inaugural medals and prepared an article about them for the *Washington Star,* which at my suggestion was run under Joe McGaraghy's name to make sure it got printed.

During my research, I had gone to the main D.C. library—then located at Mt. Vernon Square—and found they had a fine collection of early inaugural medals loose in a shoe box. After studying and listing the contents, I returned the box, without giving it much more thought. Sometime later, as a matter of curiosity, I returned to the library and asked to see the box again, only to be told it had been stolen.

Goldwater and the Southern Republican Party

In 1964, I went to my third Republican convention, in San Francisco, where Barry Goldwater was nominated as the Republican candidate to oppose Lyndon Johnson.

At the time of the 1952 Republican Convention in Chicago there was, it should be remembered, absolutely no real Republican Party south of the Mason-Dixon line. In order to win national elections, Republicans had to take most of the states in the North. It should also be remembered that during the Eisenhower-Taft contest in 1952 in Chicago, the nomination had turned on the seating of delegates from Texas and Louisiana. As there were really no organized Republican parties in the South, and they never had primaries, the parties were in the hands of a few people, and as a result it often happened that two or more groups showed up at the convention and the Credentials Committee had to meet and decide which delegation should be seated.

I was then active in the National Young Republican organization, and as a group we vowed that a real Republican Party had to be created in the South. At San Francisco in 1964, this finally came to pass. However, it turned out to be not at all what I wanted to see. What we got in the South was a switch of the younger, brighter, and more able politicians from the old Southern Democratic Party to take charge of the new Southern Republican Party. Be careful what you wish for.

I had wished for a Southern Republican Party, imagining that it would have the same values as the Republican Party of the days of Taft, Warren, and Dewey. But what we got was a vigorous, bright, and aggressive Southern Republican Party that had all the aims and goals of the solid South of the Democratic Party.

In San Francisco in 1964, they appeared full of vigor and strength, demanded and got the nomination of Barry Goldwater and a platform that echoed their values. Rockefeller was booed off the speaker's rostrum, and even Ronald Reagan, who made his first attempt at a presidential campaign that year, was shunted aside, even though he was the governor of what was to become the country's largest state. (Actually, Barry Goldwater was a personally delightful person, and afterwards, we often met when he would visit General and Betty Quinn on the Eastern Shore near our home outside of St. Michaels.)

The only delightful thing that happened to me in San Francisco was seeing my first topless dancer. Carl Shipley, a friend of his named Bill, and

I crowded into a night club. Bill had a fireman's pass that he used to get us into the show. The topless dancer came down riding a circle cut out of the ceiling. All I could say was—wow!

John Lindsay and the New York Mayoral Election of 1965

After the 1964 Goldwater-Johnson presidential campaign, the Republican Party was at its lowest ebb. I was the finance chairman of the District of Columbia Republican Party at the time, and Goldwater was so unpopular that when I was out fund raising, people would cross the street in order to avoid meeting me. After the '64 election, I even attended a very somber meeting of the Republican National Committee (RNC) in Chicago on Inauguration Day when Lyndon Johnson was sworn in. We met at one of Chicago's big downtown hotels, and it was icy, cold, and foggy outside. The temperature inside at the meeting of the RNC was about the same. That we elected my good friend Ray Bliss chairman of the Republican Party was about the only good thing that happened to us Republicans in 1965.

The assembled party had elected Ray by a standing ovation, after which a committee was formed to go to Ray and bring him in to the hall so he could be declared the new national chairman. It took so long for him to come in that just before he did, one wag, expressing the disaster that was 1964, said, "Maybe Ray Bliss decided not to accept."

Not only was Ray the best thing to happen to the party in that year, he was the best thing that happened to it for the next three years. During that time he completely made over the Republican Party, and in the process paved the way for Richard Nixon's election in 1968. But the first thing Nixon did after getting elected was to fire Ray Bliss!

The second thing he did was to fire Bernbaum. Maury, the husband of my cousin Betty Hahn, had been our ambassador to Venezuela as well as several other South and Central American countries. Against Maury's advice, Nixon had made an ill-advised trip to one of the South American countries and was so badly treated that citizens spat on him. Perversely, he blamed Maury, who'd been assigned by the State Department to accompany him, and he fired him as ambassador.

In 1965, however, all of that was ahead of us. At the nadir of the party's fortunes, I decided to see if I could encourage some of the brighter—and more moderate—Republicans to run for office. When I learned that my good friend and former classmate John Lindsay was challenging Abe Beame, the incumbent Democratic mayor of New York, Margot and I moved up there to help. We made a reservation at the Stanhope, an old hotel that catered to travelers from Europe and was located across the street from the Metropolitan Museum of Art. When the hotel learned that we were there to campaign for John Lindsay, they gave us such a ridiculously low rate that we stayed there for almost a month, the entire time we were there.

Knowing of my background in fund raising, the Lindsay campaign set me to work raising money from Republicans around the country. This turned out to be easier than I had anticipated because the rest of the party obviously felt the same way I did and wanted to give John a hand. The Lindsay family, all of whom were involved in the campaign, were most gracious and treated us beautifully. They invited us to their house on Long Island and included us as often as possible in the fun and interesting things that were taking place in the campaign. I've always loved all of them, including John's wife, Mary, and his older brother, whose wife was also named Mary, aka "Phony Mary," and John's younger brother, Roddy, who was a rising star at one of the big banks in New York and whose wife was a dog fancier and important in dog show circles. And finally there was John's twin brother, David, who was also a good friend and former classmate of mine.

To me, one of the fascinating things about New York mayoral politics was the way they pronounced the name of the election—everybody called it the "Morality Contest"! The irony of that mispronunciation was that the New York election process, which I'd said had "hair on its chest," was anything but moral. As far back as Fiorello LaGuardia, New York Democrats, always the ruling party, had hair on their chests. For example, one of the things they did for fun and games whenever there was a good-sized Lindsay rally anywhere in Manhattan was to call out the fire department and arrange for fire engines to run through the campaign rally and break it up.

Another fascinating aspect of the campaign was that one of the Lindsay brothers would take us on late night visits to the various clubhouses. I was unaware that clubhouses still existed in New York, but they not only existed as part of Tammany Hall but as part of the Republican scene as well. (I recently read a very good book about Teddy Roosevelt that said when he started in Republican politics in New York some seventy years ago, Republican clubhouses were already in existence.)

At the time of the Lindsay race, the biggest Republican vote-getter was Senator Jacob Javits, and he spent enormous amounts of time working hard and campaigning for John in the city.

Of all the fascinating things that happened in that campaign, perhaps the most fascinating was what happened on election day itself. From out of the blue, Bob Sweet, who was helping run the campaign (and is now a Federal District Court judge in New York City) called me in and gave me instructions to go up to 125th Street in Harlem on election morning and run the Republican headquarters there. I had never done anything even remotely exciting (in politics) before.

I was told to expect that the Democrats would disable the voting machines in the precincts that seemed strongly disposed to John Lindsay. As I understood it, the Democrat captain in each precinct would go in first and put a pin somewhere in the machine, and then pull the crank, which would disable it temporarily. The point was that Republican voters who were backed up in line behind the first voter would get tired of waiting for the machine to be fixed and would go home—without voting. If and when a Republican captain reported that this had happened, I was supposed to jump on the telephone and report that the machines were down at Precinct Number so-and-so. Then I was to notify an organization that had been set up by the Lindsay people that would send over some entertainers—monkey acts, dog acts, guitar players, jugglers, and so forth—from their bank of hundreds, to entertain the Republicans, i.e., Lindsay voters, who were still waiting in line.

Sure enough, as soon as the polls opened, the reports of machines being disabled with Lindsay voters lined up waiting to vote began to come in. So I then did as Bob Sweet had told me to do, I yelled and screamed over the phone at the Election Commission—and then called for the entertainers.

That night, we went to Lindsay's campaign headquarters at the Roosevelt Hotel (which he called his good luck hotel) and joined the crowd awaiting the election returns. In the early evening, the returns were very bleak. Beame was running far ahead, and the computers, basing their evaluation on these early returns, had already predicted a landslide victory for Abe Beame. Margot and I were so dispirited by what was happening that we snuck out of the good luck hotel and went back to the Stanhope where we got in bed and watched the returns on television. Then, all of a sudden, at about one or two in the morning, the whole tide turned. All excited, we got dressed by jumping into our clothes and got a taxi back to Lindsay headquarters so that we'd be there when John accepted his election.

What had happened was that despite the broken machines, the Lindsay voters stayed in line and waited until they could vote, even if the polls closed. They could do this because in New York, as in a number of other cities, at the close of polling, a policeman gets in the end of the line. Everyone in front of him gets to vote, no matter how long it takes, but no more people can get in line behind him. As a result, a great number of pro-Lindsay votes began to come in *after* midnight, and because so many Lindsay polling places all over the city had similarly disabled voting machines, the computers had been fooled by the one-sided information that had come in earlier, so the flood of Lindsay votes that came in after the polls closed produced an overwhelming victory for John. However, Lindsay's tenure as the Republican mayor did not turn out very well. Four years later, he ran and was re-elected as a Democrat.

One of John's problems was his campaign manager, Bob Price, who had run Lindsay's congressional campaigns in Manhattan's Silk Stocking district for years. A street-wise New Yorker and terrific manager, Bob had had a lot to do with John's successful campaigns for Congress, and also as an architect of his election as mayor. When John was inaugurated in January, Bob became John's deputy mayor, which is where and when the trouble began. Bob forgot that it was John who'd been elected mayor, not he, and John subsequently had to replace him.

For quite a while, we had happy times in our association with John and Mary Lindsay, who were always lovely to us and to our family. Our daughter Polly, our youngest child, a classmate of little Johnny Lindsay, got invited to a lovely week-long visit at Gracie Mansion with her pal Johnny. Unfortunately, Johnny's path through life was not a smooth one. He got involved in drug use and drug peddling, and ended up in jail. After his term as mayor, John Lindsay became a very unhappy fellow. Ultimately, he got sick and depressed, in part as a result of his son's problems, so that what had begun as a happy adventure ended on a sad note for all concerned.

Pat Buchanan and the 1976 Ford Nomination

By 1976, although I was neither City Council nor Republican Party chairman, I wrangled an invitation to the 1976 GOP Convention in Kansas City, Missouri. Unfortunately, its suspense and excitement were slight.

The excitement, such as it was, was provided by Ronald Reagan, by that point the governor of California, who was making his first serious effort to get the Republican nomination. I was interested to see, in his camp, my old friend Cliff White *and* Pat Buchanan.

No one expected anything but the nomination of Gerald Ford, who had been elected by the House as vice president to replace the disgraced Spiro Agnew, who had "resigned." When Richard Nixon resigned, Ford became president, and Nelson Rockefeller was elected vice president. Nevertheless, the conservatives had begun to feel their oats, and a Ford-Rockefeller ticket was not to their liking.

I was not surprised to see Cliff. I had known and liked him in our Young Republican days, even though we were usually on opposite sides of everything. He was always a bona fide right wing conservative, but his party skills made him well liked and respected across the board. In any case, I liked him.

Pat Buchanan was more of a surprise. I had known Pat casually when he was a speech writer for President Nixon while I was City Council chairman and made frequent visits to the White House.

Why the surprise? Nixon (compared to today's Congressional Republicans) was no right wing conservative. On the contrary, his record (leaving aside Watergate and the animosities developed in the Helen Gahagan Douglas campaign and the Alger Hiss affair decades earlier) was as far left as you could get and remain a Republican. For example, he appointed Pat Moynihan as his domestic counselor, and he carried forward and implemented Lyndon Johnson's Great Society program.

I also knew Pat as the partner of our good friend Tom Braden in their radio and then television show, "Crossfire." (But not as well as I would get to know him when Margot and I went on a tour to Egypt and Israel sponsored and led by Braden and Buchanan.) In any case, the convention acted as expected, by nominating Ford, and we left satisfied. But not Pat.

On my way out of the convention hall, I was ambling along, minding my own business, perhaps with a small smile on my face, when Pat, coming along behind me, got my attention.

In an angry and disappointed voice, he said, "Gil, you liberals are laughing now, but you'll be sorry later." Boy, was he ever right!

Pat emerged as the far right, bigoted, rabble-rouser he has now become; he left the Republican Party and tried for the nomination as the presidential candidate of the Independent Party. (He lost.)

Who knows how this will effect the Bush-Gore election in 2000.

Chapter 3

ℰᎧᏯ

... *Strange Bedfellows*

Henry Kissinger and Shoe Imports

A t about the same time that I was appointed City Council chairman by President Nixon, my father, the head of our family retail shoe business in Washington, Baltimore, and other places, sold the family business. The buyer was the United States Shoe Corporation, a major shoe manufacturer with headquarters in Cincinnati, Ohio. (Red Cross shoes were then their signature product.) Hahn's was their first venture into the retail business.

At this time, imports of all kinds were causing serious dislocations, such as loss of sales and jobs to foreign imports for a variety of large industries in this country. One of the largest industries affected by the imports was shoe manufacturing. The efficient, cheap, and easily transportable equipment for shoe-making was pouring out of countries like Germany. Factories were opening left and right in developing countries to make shoes outside the United States. They could do so much cheaper than we were making them in Kentucky, Ohio, and Indiana (the Tri-States).

Concerned about the problem, Phil Barach, the young CEO of US Shoe, became an evangelist for the goal of restricting the importation of shoes in the United States so as to protect the domestic shoe business.

The shoe industry was simultaneously working through its lobbying organization in Washington to do that very same thing. But Phil, one of the world's great salesmen, was not satisfied with what the industry reps were doing. He determined to take the matter into his own hands.

Phil was confident that as a great salesman he could sell anyone or anything, including the president of the United States, in this case Richard Nixon. Phil viewed restricting the importation of shoes into the country, therefore, saving both jobs and American industry, as "God's work."

Although I did not know the president well, I did know Henry Kissinger rather well. In fact, I'd seen quite a bit of him before he had become the Great Man. He was then a relatively minor counselor to the president, but he did have an office in the White House, and influence over things like U.S. policy on importation. Phil Barach was aware that I used to entertain meetings of the US Shoe board with tales of goings-on in Washington, about my attending morning meetings at the White House when we greeted important foreign visitors. Henry Kissinger, of course, was always there.

Phil asked me who he could see in Washington to persuade the president to restrict the import of shoes into the United States, especially from countries like Brazil. I suggested Henry.

I obtained Henry's promise to meet with Phil and to listen to Phil's pitch on restricting shoe imports, and Phil came to Washington. The three of us met in the West Wing. They talked and I listened. This went on for an hour.

At the end, we walked outside, and Phil was jubilant. Henry Kissinger, he declared, was just wonderful; he was going to persuade the president to stop the importation of all shoes into the United States. He, Phil, had saved the industry. Stunned, I was speechless for a few minutes.

Finally I said, "Phil, it's a lucky thing that you had me along as an interpreter in the ways of Washington. You may have thought you heard Henry tell you that the president was going to restrict the importation of shoes, because, I expect that's what you wanted to hear.

"But what he said was that there was no chance at all that the president was going to restrict the import of shoes. Indeed, he said that if you knew what was good for you and your industry, you'd start importing shoes yourself as a wholesaler."

It didn't take long for Phil to regain his self-possession. He went back to Cincinnati and almost immediately began cutting down the amount of manufacturing US Shoe did in the Tri-States, and purchasing manufacturers and products from Brazil, Italy, and eventually China, turning much of the company's shoe division into importing and wholesaling.

John Mitchell and I

Poor John Mitchell deserved a lot of the abuse that he got. And he got a lot. But he never got credit for some of the very nice things that he did.

I think it's fair to say that John Mitchell liked me, and that I liked him back. He was pleased by some small services that I'd been able to perform during the election of 1968, and he was everlastingly cordial to me and entirely responsible for my appointment as chairman of the City Council. Indeed, toward the end of my three-year term as chairman, he made a comment to me that I found to be revealing. He said that he was no longer in a position to "protect me." It was fair to say that I was startled to learn that I had needed protection—and therefore surprised that his protection was coming to an end.

Later, looking back on the matter, I could understand what had happened (and why) and realized that Mitchell was anticipating a disaster himself. I have always taken it kindly that he took the time to be worried about my small matters when he himself was, so to speak, gazing into the pit. I guess I had not appreciated the skills it took to be a bond counsel.

It turned out that John Mitchell shared my passion for cities. His work as bond counsel in his New York firm had made him an expert in housing, transportation, city financing, hospitals, and welfare, all of the skills that it takes to make a city work.

It was John Mitchell who steered me to the solution to the subway problem, and encouraged my opposition to the completion of the interstate freeway system through the city and the building of the Three Sisters Bridge. And he provided the suggestion that steered me to the $200 million we needed to get the subway construction underway (no pun intended). He gave constant advice regarding the plans I had for housing construction in the city, as well as for bus services, and suggestions for improving police and fire services. Interestingly, since Mitchell continued to nurture his "bad cop" image, he never let anyone know, during his lifetime, of all the good things he did for cities. But the other side of him enjoyed, vicariously, the several successes that I enjoyed in doing things to help the District of Columbia.

His door was always open to me, and no subject involving cities was out of bounds in our various discussions. No urban problem existed that he didn't know about and have a way to fix. He was constantly taking my side when the solutions I proposed (often suggested by him) were met with opposition at the White House. On another playing field, I consider that he served this city and this country very well during the troubled period from 1969 to 1972.

As I mention in another story, for a while there it seemed there was a riot or demonstration, or both, nearly every weekend in Washington. It is not much of an exaggeration to say that some weekends we were very close to a revolution on the streets.

In preparation for the worst of these weekends—like Mobilization Day to protest the Vietnam War—Mitchell would hold a meeting in his office. I was always there, as were the mayor, the military representatives, the various police chiefs, Interior Department security, and many others involved in security, health, and safety. We gathered to make plans to cope.

What Mitchell laid down for Mobilization Day was so successful that it ought to be more widely known. Mitchell put forward the following simple program: the protesters were to be welcomed, encouraged to have their say; nobody was to get hurt; and when it was time to go, they were to leave. As I recall, nobody got hurt; they all had their say; and by Sunday they left town.

Simple and successful, thanks to John Mitchell—a far nicer man than he was given credit for being.

General Vernon Walters and His Memory

In a later story, I relate how much Margot and I enjoyed going through the receiving line ceremony at the White House receptions held on the south lawn for heads of state and prime ministers. As far as we were concerned, this was one of the nicest "perks" of the job of City Council chairman and "City Father." The ceremony always took the form of the Home Team and the Visiting Team, with the dignitaries standing to one side prior to a review of one of the Washington ceremonial troops by the president and the visiting dignitary. Then there would be a welcoming speech by the president, followed by a response from the visiting fireman.

Usually, the head of state or prime minister spoke in his own language with a "translator" standing behind him. This person would either read the message from a prepared text, or he'd take the impromptu remarks down in shorthand and read them off in English a few moments later.

But that's not the way it happened in the case of President Nixon and General Vernon Walters, a great big burly but handsome man who stood at attention, in his general's uniform, directly behind President Nixon.

President Nixon was very good at this sort of thing. He usually delivered his welcoming speech *ex-tempore*. General Walters, who was fluent in as many as twenty different languages, would stand there with no prepared text, no shorthand book, memorizing the speech in English then he would give back the speech in the language of the visiting president, king, or prime minister!

This was always, to say the least, a very impressive performance. The scene shifts now to the live television coverage of the Senate Watergate hearings in 1974. General Walters, now the number two man at the CIA, was called before the committee because of the suspected involvement of the CIA in the Watergate matter.

After giving his name, rank, and serial number to the Senate, General Walters was asked his first substantive question.

General Walters replied: "I don't remember, Senator."

I Get Fired by Haldeman and Erlichman

Nobody likes to be fired. But if you *are* fired, it always helps to be fired by experts. I was fairly ambivalent at the end of the third year of my term as to whether or not to take another one. While I thoroughly enjoyed being chairman and had a lot of fun, I had given all of my time to the job. I'd had a couple of overtures to give up the City Council and take an ambassadorship, but was quite certain this would involve a tent somewhere on the east coast of Africa. (I don't think I was deceiving myself about that.) Another overture involved the possibility of a Federal judgeship, but I didn't think that was likely. The one thing I would have liked that didn't come my way was a high post in the Justice Department. So, having no hope of that, I was turning over and discussing in my mind and with Margot whether or not to serve another term or to give it up and go back to practicing law.

Then, out of the blue, came a telephone call summoning me to the White House. Presidential Assistant Egil ("Bud") Krogh said, "Gil, we've got to go in and talk to Haldeman and Erlichman about your reappointment and I want you, for once, to pay attention and be serious." Haldeman said, "Hahn, we're willing to reappointment you as chairman, but as you know there's an election coming up this year, and we don't want any more shit out of you." The answer popped out of my mouth before I could stop it: "Then get yourself another boy." And they did.

There was a sad denouement to this story. Some years later, after Bud Krogh got out of jail, I had a chance meeting with him while walking across Lafayette Park. We stopped to exchange handshakes, and as we parted, Krogh said, "Gil, I've often wished that I had paid more attention to the things you had to say."

Good Bedfellows Make Strange Politicians

Not too many months after returning to private life, I took on, for the Republican State Committee, the job of running a fund-raising dinner to support the reelection of President Richard Nixon. I had no animus toward the president; in fact, I thought he'd had an excellent first term, and as a lifelong Republican, I was pleased to support his reelection. Indeed, as a politician myself I could not quarrel with the wisdom of not reappointing me, so I also had no animus toward Haldeman or Erlichman, or Krogh for that matter.

Margot, however, who is made of sterner stuff, promptly joined the McGovern campaign. Soon she was tooling around the country in the company of Eleanor McGovern, even flying in small airplanes, which she hates to do. I might forgive and forget, but not Margot. This contretemps titillated the local press, and the day before the fund-raising dinner, it was the subject of a piece of gossip in the *Washington Star* by Betty Beale, then the most-read gossip columnist of the Washington papers (though Maxine Cheshire of the *Washington Post* might have disagreed).

Betty Beale reported that on the very night there was to be a fund-raising dinner for the president chaired by myself, my wife was bombing around the country with Eleanor McGovern working *against* the election of Mr. Nixon. That night, as I got ready to introduce Elliott Richardson, the featured speaker of the evening, I gazed down in front of me and there was Betty Beale at the first table.

"Ladies and Gentlemen," I said, "you probably read in the *Star* that Betty Beale reported that while I am running this dinner tonight, my wife Margot is out tooling around the country with Eleanor McGovern seeking the president's defeat. This is what I have to say about the matter: It only goes to prove that good bedfellows make strange politicians. Ladies and Gentlemen, Elliot Richardson."

I was very pleased with the thunderous applause that greeted my comment, and as Elliott stepped past me to the microphone, he said, "Gil, how do you expect me to go on after an introduction like *that*?" Margot, when she heard about my comment, said only, "You wish."

Richard Nixon and the Tax Deduction (1974)

Don't misunderstand me, Richard Nixon was not a very nice man. Nonetheless, I owed him a good deal. One of the most enjoyable parts of my career came from his appointing me chairman of the City Council of the District of Columbia. I have noted elsewhere of the kind of help that the city and I received at the hands of John Mitchell, Nixon's close friend and attorney general, especially in the matter of stopping the freeways from coming through the city and funding the start of the subway.

This story has to do with the tapes and Richard Nixon's impeachment. Two events combined to bring this back to mind. First, as I write this, William Jefferson Clinton is faced with an impeachment proceeding of his own. Second, the newspaper tells us that Mr. Nixon's estate is suing the United States for over $200 million for the tapes that the Government kept and would not return.

When the matter of the tapes first surfaced, being a Republican and grateful Nixon adherent, I wished him out of the difficulties he was in. So, I day-dreamed about what the president ought to do about the tapes. This is the scenario.

Mr. Nixon sets up an interview for the television audience in prime time. Behind his chair is a roaring fire in a White House fireplace. Nixon speaks: "Ladies and Gentlemen, citizens of the country. It is true that we kept a taping system in the White House. In fact, I inherited it from the previous administration. All of my most intimate interviews and discussions have been recorded. The only purpose of this record was for the book or books I planned to write after I left office at the end of this second term.

"A request that I do not wish to honor has been made for these tapes. In honor, I cannot release them, and this is the reason. All of my most confidential talks with heads of foreign governments and their ambassadors and ministers are on these tapes. It is not in the national interest to release their private talks with your president.

"So, if you will watch the fire behind my chair, you will see all of the tapes going up in smoke to protect all of our interests as Americans."

This would have been so easy. Why wasn't it done?

Here's my theory. At just about the same time, the papers of former Vice President Hubert Humphrey were allowed a tax deduction to Mr. Humphrey when he donated them to the University of Minnesota. As a result of this gift and the tax deduction, the IRS issued a brand new ruling: no further gifts of papers from an officer of the United States is hereafter entitled to a tax deduction.

I fantasized that Mr. Nixon, a good lawyer, noted that the ruling did not say "and tapes." The value of the tapes (presumably $200 million) would have saved the Nixon family from paying taxes for the rest of his life.

Pat Buchanan

One may not like Pat Buchanan's politics or the prejudices he sometimes displays (and Margot and I don't), but there's no denying the fact that he is one of the funniest individuals on the planet.

Pat has been a friend of ours for years, though not as long as Pat's former political sparring partner, Tom Braden, and Tom's late wife, Joan. In their heyday and while at the top of their form, Pat and Tom had the best radio talk show in Washington. "Crossfire," which was on every afternoon, featured the most interesting guests talking about the most intriguing topics. They kicked everything (and everyone) around, Pat from the right and Tom from the left of the political spectrum.

The afternoon show was so popular that congressmen who happened to be listening to it while driving would pull over, hurry to a pay phone (only the very rich had phones in their cars in those pre-cell phone days), and call in their own commentary. The show stirred *that* much interest. I was a guest several times while City Council chairman and enjoyed myself thoroughly each and every time. Later, the show moved to television, but for me it never held the same kick as the no-holds-barred radio show.

Their fame became so great that one summer a local travel agency asked them to lead a tour of Egypt and Israel. The wonders of the Nile and religious spots in Israel would be interspersed with periodic lectures from Tom and Pat. The minute we heard about the tour, Margot and I signed up for it, and we never had a better time.

Starting with Cairo and the Pyramids, the Hahns and the Bradens took a side trip, away from the group, on a boat that went up the Nile to such wondrous places as the Valley of the Kings, Luxor, the Temple of Karnak, and the tomb of Queen Hatshepsut. Pat, who was left to lead the rest of the tour on his own, let us know he considered our stranding him in that manner a serious breach of friendship, and neither forgave us nor ever let us forget it.

At the time of this trip, the Israelis still controlled one-third of the Sinai Desert (they would later give it back to Egypt), which made our journey by bus to Jerusalem from Cairo rather interesting. As the Israelis were still in partial control of the desert, the Egyptians were being nice to them, one of the results of which was that on the last boat trip up the Nile, there were quite a few Israelis, even some former soldiers, enjoying Egypt. No more, alas.

The trip across the Sinai from Egypt's two-thirds to the Israeli-held sector took just over two hours. In the Egyptian portion, all one could see was desert, plus a few camels and hundreds of burnt-out tanks. But once we reached the Israeli zone, the countryside was lush. Everything was green and growing, and there were cattle revolving under water showers. I imagine now that the Egyptians once again have the entire area, the whole landscape is desert.

Although we had been promised accommodations in the King David Hotel, we ended up at a hotel in East Jerusalem. From there we journeyed out to see holy places in Bethlehem and Jerico, where we were forced to eat the atrocious Israeli food. One day Margot found a limo and a driver who turned out to be the uncle of a Palestinian friend of ours in Washington, Issa Howar. Would he take us on a tour of Israeli points of interest *and* find us some Palestinian food? He said he would be happy to do so, and proceeded to introduce us to wonderful food at hole-in-the-wall places behind gas stations and near Good Fence, which is next to Syria in the Golan Heights, and Jerico and Bethlehem, to name just a few.

Once again, the Bradens and the Hahns left Pat Buchanan behind, and once again we had a fine time.

Many years later, after Pat had run for the presidency on the Independent ticket, he and Tom had lunch together. According to Tom, Pat said that in the latter stages of the 2000 campaign he began to lose sleep at night worrying about the possibility that he might take enough votes away from George Bush to swing the election to Al Gore. But, he told Tom, he stopped worrying because God came to him during the night and told him not to worry. God said, "Don't fret. I have it arranged that all your Jewish friends in Miami-Dade County will vote for Bush." Then God took Pat by the wrist and said, "However, I want your promise that you'll never do shit like this [running for President] again!"

According to Tom, Pat said that he did, in fact, cost Bush the electoral votes in three states. But I never checked that out.

Goldwater

General William Quinn, a very distinguished WWII general, whom we came to know in Easton on Maryland's Eastern Shore, was part of the Seventh Army invasion of Southern France. A graduate of West Point, where he'd starred in lacrosse, he had been, in between the end of the OSS and the creation of the CIA, in charge of the National Intelligence Agency. (For the record, he was also, and not incidentally, the father of Sally Quinn, *Washington Post* columnist and wife of Ben Bradlee, the *Post*'s executive editor emeritus.)

During Goldwater's presidential campaign in 1964, Gen. Quinn, a good friend of the senator's, was serving as commander-in-chief of the U.S. armed forces in Germany, which was protecting Western Europe from a potential Russian invasion. Senator Goldwater paid his friend a visit in Germany, and while he was there, he made a campaign speech that was quite critical of President Lyndon Johnson. Shortly thereafter, Gen. Quinn was replaced.

Chapter 4

ဢဢ

People and Places

Lanier Place and Horse Racing

Every Sunday when I was a child, I would go straight from Sunday School to the midday brunch at my grandparents, the Kings, on Lanier Place, northwest Washington. I looked forward to these gatherings with great anticipation, and I was never disappointed.

Lanier Place is a side street at one end of what is now called Adams-Morgan, the area centered around 18th and Columbia Road. Today, the neighborhood is well known for its many ethnic restaurants and has been, in the decades since I was a regular visitor, first an all-Black neighborhood and now an almost entirely Latino one. In the 1920s, however, Lanier Place was simply a quiet street in a quiet neighborhood east of Rock Creek Park— *and* the Center of the Washington Jewish community.

Brunch at the Kings was held on a big round table in the center of a large dining room under the pleasant glow of a huge green Tiffany lamp. Nearby was the ever-present telephone, a "stand-up" model that had been specially equipped with a forty-foot cord so that the phone could be passed around the full length of the table (everyone knew they could reach any of my family members there on any Sunday).

For me, one of the major attractions was that my three bachelor uncles still lived in the house. They all still lived upstairs on the third and fourth floors. I always knew they'd be around, and they'd be talking sports. The family was definitely into sports.

My great-uncle Phil King had been a star quarterback at Princeton around 1900. In fact, he'd made Grantland Rice's All-American team *and* his All-Time team. Uncle Phil, who played with Baltimore's famous Poe brothers, is still considered one of Princeton's greatest stars. My uncle Sylvan, who'd been an outstanding star at Washington's Central High School, was a star in his freshman year at Princeton and seemed to have an unlimited future there—until he flunked out. My Uncle Henry played center for Virginia, and my great uncle Sam had been a track star. They all also starred in baseball.

The conversation at Sunday brunch was so entertaining that friends and even distant relatives would arrive to take seats behind the diners and just listen. The talk at the table was restricted to four topics: pro baseball, college football, prize-fighting, and horse racing. No politics, no religion, or anything else. Just those sports.

Uncle Sylvan was considered the "lover boy." When he got phone calls, he would take the phone into a closet so that no one else could hear him talk to his girls.

My uncle Milton, a bon vivant lawyer, was much later the attorney for George Preston Marshall, owner of the Washington Redskins and laundry mogol (he owned the Palace Laundry). Uncle Milton had a 5% ownership interest in the Redskins. Thanks to him and to Uncle Sylvan, the family always had 50-yard-line seats at the old Griffith Stadium, which was in my opinion the best place ever to watch an NFL game.

Uncle Sylvan wanted to buy another 5% of the Redskins for himself, but Milton talked him out of it, telling him it was too risky. Had Uncle Sylvan ignored his advice and gone ahead, by the year 2000 that stock would have been worth $90 million. When Milton died, my cousin Bob Frank sold Milton's Redskins stock to Jack Kent Cooke for less than $1,000,000. I begged him to keep it—or to sell it to me—but he wouldn't.

My lifelong interest in sports of all kinds was kindled by this family background. I played some baseball and football, without fame or fortune, but I never stopped enjoying it.

My interest in horse racing was fanned by my grandfather, who from time to time would take me to the racetrack in Bowie, Maryland, along with J. Edgar Hoover and Clyde Tolson. My grandfather would let me cash in his winning tickets and bring him back the cash.

For years and years, I wanted to own a professional sports team, but I never had near enough money to do so. Then, many years later, I got hooked on horse racing, mainly through reading Dick Francis's novels about horse racing in England, and I came to see that anyone could own a race horse. So I set out to create a racing stable in Maryland. The attached article from *Maryland Horse* magazine explains how that turned out. While it may have not been a monetary success, it was certainly an artistic one, and great fun. At one point, we even owned a filly in England (called Shortening Bread). She won one race. While Margot loved racing in England, she hated it in Maryland, and was delighted when I gave it up.

An article written about my horse racing days in *Maryland Horse*:

Meeting House Farm Is Winning Combination
(story by Lucy Acton)

Calumet Farm had Ben A. Jones. Eugene Klein has D. Wayne Lukas. Here in Maryland, in much the same tradition, Gilbert Hahn, Jr. dominates the claiming owner's ranks with trainer Tom Caviness.

Hahn, a prominent Washington D.C. attorney, got into the horse business a little less than five years ago. Since then, he has been Maryland's leading owner in races won for four years in a row. Between January 1 and October 31, 1987 (the last period for which statistics are available) his Meeting House Farm had 61 victories—exactly 20 more than the next-leading Maryland-based owner, King T. Leatherbury's Jim Stable.

Owner-trainer matches aren't made in heaven—but Hahn and Caviness will tell you they have one of the best to be found on earth. "Tommy is polite enough to ask my opinion on things," says Hahn, with the warm grin that is trademark of a contented owner. He has served as Chairman of the City Council in Washington D.C., and has also been chairman of the board of two major Washington hospitals. But when it comes to his racing stable, Mr. Hahn looks to his trainer to make the decisions. "Sometimes I have an opinion. But I'm not an expert. He is."

Caviness' skills as a handicapper are the single most important element in their operation. A former exercise boy who has spent most of his adult life on the racetrack, Caviness came to the realization years ago that "there is more to training horses than galloping and working and racing. You have got to know what they are worth. And the only way to figure out what a horse is worth is through handicapping."

The trainer compares his approach to playing the stock market. "You speculate," explains Caviness, who has no other clients besides Hahn. Meeting House Farm carries 30 to 35 horses in training year-round, and there is tremendous turnover in their barn. "A lot of times you overpay," he admits. "Then you go on to the next one."

Caviness has read all the books on handicapping, and he follows speed figures, but he also uses his own intuition. "Being here in the afternoon, to watch the races and look at the horses in the paddock, is about 50 percent of it." he says.

What are some of the factors that influence the decision to claim or not to claim? "It depends on the age of the horse," Caviness says. "Most 2-year-olds are running for inflated prices. So you have to be careful. I watch the horse run, and examine his legs and physique.

Racing has always held an attraction for Mr. Hahn. "When I was a child, and we would go for visits with my (maternal) grandparents, there were only four subjects ever discussed at the Sunday morning breakfast table," he says. "Those were prize fighting, professional baseball, college football, and horse racing." Hahn is the fourth generation of his family to live in Washington, and his connections with politics and government run deep. He is the first member of his family to own horses, however. "My mother's father used to come to Bowie and Laurel years ago with J. Edgar Hoover," he says. "But he never actually owned any himself."

Hahn went to Phillips Exeter Academy and Princeton, and is a distinguished veteran of World War II. A forward observer in the field artillery, he served in Patton's Army, and was involved on the Normandy landings. Wounded in the campaign at Metz, Hahn was on his way to the Pacific to join the U.S. forces there when the bomb was dropped on Hiroshima.

After the War, he enrolled in Yale Law School, with the goal of becoming involved in politics, and eventually he founded his own law firm, Amram & Hahn, in Washington. For many years, Mr. Hahn served on the Republican National Committee. He headed the City Council in Washington from 1969 to 1972.

Hahn has also donated his time to many volunteer causes, including the Washington Hospital Center and the city's D.C. General Hospital, where he was chairman of the board for five years.

It was soon after his term at D.C. General expired in the early 1970s that Hahn became involved in racing. "I had been a fan of (racing novelist) Dick Francis for years," he explains. "But it had never occurred to me that anybody could own horses—that you didn't have to be born into it. I was looking around for another side interest and all of a sudden the idea came to me.

"Once I'd decided to become an owner, I had to have a trainer. Just about that time, Andy Beyer wrote a piece in the *Washington Post* about Tom Caviness. I called the racetrack and the racing secretary, Larry Abbundi, arranged for Tommy and me to have an appointment to meet. Whatever success I've had since then has been all due to Tommy."

Caviness was already on his way up when he and Hahn met, in the spring of 1983. He had been one of the leading trainers at the Bowie winter meeting with a modest string of claiming horses, and he led the trainer's standings for the first 60 days at the Pimlico meeting, with a public stable of only 12 horses, but he had never trained more than a dozen horses at a time before getting together with Hahn.

Although results came quickly, by almost any standard, once Meeting House Farm got rolling, Caviness says he took it relatively slowly in the beginning. "It took us about two and a half months to find the right horse—one that we wouldn't just be throwing money away on," he recalls. The first horse he bought for Mr. Hahn was a filly at the Maryland State Agency's Two-Year-Olds in Training sale that May. Named Margot H. (after Mr. Hahn's wife), the filly cost $17,000. She was unsound, and unlucky. But that fall, Hahn was to get lucky with a colt named Northern Pass, whom Caviness claimed for him at Laurel for $25,000. Within a month, Northern Pass won for Hahn in allowance company, and the following year he became Hahn's first stakes winner with a victory in the All Maryland handicap at Timonium.

Hahn named his racing stable Meeting House Farm after a property which he owns, Meetinghouse Cove, on the Eastern Shore.

Caviness began training exclusively for Hahn in 1984 and settled easily into the role of a private trainer. "It gave me my first real opportunity to do things the way I wanted to do them," he comments. "When you're dealing with a lot of different owners, and they all have different expectations, it's a whole different life."

Caviness grew up in South Baltimore and, like his boss, had only slight contact with racing as a child. His father, and various other members of his family, worked in a clothing factory. "My father liked to play horses. When I was 14 or 15, a friend of my father's got me a job working at Delaware Park one summer with Billy Christmas," he says.

A high school dropout at the age of 17, Caviness completed his schooling in the army, while he was stationed in Germany a few years later. His first job after getting out of the army at 21 was a clerk and timekeeper for the Pittsburgh-Des Moines Steel Company. He soon quit that and went to work as a clerk for a trucking company. But he just wasn't happy working in an office.

"I decided I wanted to be a jockey," says Caviness, who is slightly built, but taller than many race riders. "I was 22 years old, and it had been years since I'd spent that summer at Delaware Park, but I got a job with Billy Boniface, and I learned how to ride up on his farm. A year or so later, I went to the racetrack as a freelance exercise boy."

Over the next few years, Caviness struggled with his goal of becoming a jockey. "I left three or four times, but I kept coming back. Finally, the last time, I decided to give it one last try. Then I realized I was too heavy to be a jockey—I was just kidding myself. So I went to work for Richard Dutrow as an exercise boy." Caviness stayed with Dutrow, galloping horses and working his way up to assistant trainer, before going out on his won in 1975. He supported himself as a public trainer for eight years, but he downplays any success he may have had before meeting up with Mr. Hahn. "He deserves all the recognition," in Caviness' words.

Mr. Hahn, who says he would have bought a football or baseball team had he been able to afford one, takes great pleasure in watching his horses run in the afternoons. But he rarely—if ever—shows up at Caviness' barn in the mornings, and most weekends are devoted to his family. He lives with his wife, Margot, in downtown Washington. Margot Hahn also operates a widely known private cooking school out of their home. The couple has three grown children, all living in New York City: Gilbert Hahn III, an attorney; Amanda, who is vice president of a large advertising agency; and Polly, who has just started out her career in advertising.

Hahn's life is busy, but that hasn't kept him from finding time for one more activity. The owner has been active with the new horsemen's group that replaces the local HBPA, the Maryland Thoroughbred Horsemen's Association, and last fall was elected vice president of the finance committee of the MTHA. "Unlike a lot of horsemen, and other owners, I have had a lot of experience running organizations," notes Hahn. "I thought this would be a good way for me to contribute—and learn a lot about racing at the same time. That has proved to be the case . . . . I've always liked to give something back, to help out where I can . . . . I've always enjoyed that sort of thing."

Phil King, the Princeton All-American

Back around the turn of the century, Jews were seldom admitted and not particularly welcome at Princeton, with one notable exception, my great-uncle Phil King. My mother's side of the family was filled with great athletes (my mother was an excellent athlete herself), but the greatest of them all was clearly Phil King. In those days, Princeton made no bones about its team being made up of professionals. My uncle Phil, who had been heavily recruited for his skills as a quarterback, played so well for Princeton that no less a sports authority than Grantland Rice chose Phil as his all-time choice for quarterback.

Under the leadership of Uncle Phil, Princeton's team, which also included Baltimore's famous Poe brothers, dominated the eastern college football scene. Back then the interest in college football was so intense that games like Harvard-Princeton or Yale-Princeton were the equivalent of today's Super Bowl, and easily filled such huge stadiums as New York's Polo Grounds.

After his playing days were over, Phil stayed on to coach at Princeton and later Wisconsin, after which he went into business with his brother—my maternal grandfather—Harry King. Their department store on 7th Street in Northwest Washington was called Kings Palace.

So famous was Uncle Phil that eventually there were three other Phil Kings in the extended family. First was his son Phil King, whom we called New York Phil #1. A larger than life character, he became, among other things, a prospector for gold in Mexico in the days of Pancho Villa, and fortunately, lived to tell about it. His son, New York Phil #2, was at Princeton the same time I was. In fact, we both got in courtesy of the great Phil King, whose memory lived on for generations. While New York Phil #2 was a great friend, I didn't see much of him later in life because he moved to Holland and worked as a representative of an American cosmetics company. As for the third Phil King, he was known as North Carolina Phil because he lived and worked on the outer banks of that state.

One last Princetonian memory: when I entered Princeton I went out for the freshman football team, one of whose assistant coaches was Nat Poe, who'd been my uncle Phil's teammate and friend. Nat was very excited about my connection to his great friend . . . . Until he saw me play.

Milton King and Bob Frank

My uncle Milton King was the star of his generation in my mother's family, and I was always drawn to him. A classic bon vivant, a great storyteller, and a much sought after master of ceremonies and after-dinner speaker who was gifted with a quick wit, he was very popular. The fact that he was a lawyer was a large part of the reason I decided to become one.

When he reached eighty, he liked to say, "I'm eighty years old and I don't have an enemy in the world because I've outlived all the bastards." Or, "I'm not as smart as God, but I'm as smart as God was at my age."

Milton was, among other things, attorney for George Preston Marshall, the laundry king who owned the Washington Redskins, and who eventually sold Milton first a 5 and then a 10% interest in the team. As bachelors, he and George Marshall were great ladies men and good-time fellows around town.

Late in life, Milton married Louise Berliner Frank, thereby acquiring a stepson in Bob Frank. Bob and I treated one another as cousins, and I thought he was the best thing since sliced bread. When he and his widowed mother had lived in Switzerland, he'd attended French schools and thus came to Washington with a surface sophistication that made me idolize him.

We were the best of friends until his untimely death. His burial in Arlington National Cemetery was arranged by Milton's good friend, Chief Justice Warren Burger. During World War II, Bob was an air force pilot in the China-Burma theater while I was serving in the third army in Europe.

My friend Cora Anne Berliner, who was Bob's actual cousin, and I drove down to North Carolina to attend Bob's graduation from North Carolina. On the way down, we got caught in a speed trap in Petersburg, near Richmond.

The officer who pulled us over said, in a deep Virginia drawl, "Excuse me, where you goin', Sir?" Foolishly, I said, "We're going to Chapel Hill, North Carolina, to see our cousin graduate." "No you all ain't, Sir," he replied. "You're coming to the court house with me." $50 later, we were released and allowed to go on.

When Bob and his new wife, Kitsy, came up to Princeton to visit me for house party weekends, Bob often arrived wearing his fly-boy uniform and his twenty-mission crush hat. He was the sensation of the weekend. (This was in 1942, and I was graduating a year early so I could get into the army.)

Bob's mother, Louise, came from the Berliner family. His grandfather, Emile Berliner, was a semi-famous inventor, who'd come from Germany as a youth to apprentice to Alexander Graham Bell. Later, on his own, he invented the turntable for the Victrola and the matrix for the records to be played on it. As a result, the family was loaded with RCA stock.

Louise's brother Henry Berliner was also rather famous, in his case for developing and building the Aircoupe, a small plane that could be flown using a steering wheel like an automobile, instead of a "joy stick." The factory was in Riverdale, Maryland. Uncle Milton was great friends with Hap Arnold (later General Arnold), Touey Spaatz, and Pete Quesada—all captains, lieutenants then, and his fellow members, along with Henry Berliner, of the Double Martini Club.

Milton's favorite story involved his former friend Eddie Rheem, the son-in-law of Harry Wardman, whom my mother once declared the handsomest man in Washington. Eddie was a partner in the mortgage banking firm of Schwartzle, Rheem, and Hennessey, which sold mortgages. Unfortunately, because they sold the same mortgage at least twice, Judge Letts sent Eddie Rheem to the D.C. prison at Occoquan.

When Milton went to the jail to visit his friend, he asked if there was anything he could do for him, and Eddie replied, "Call the Chevy Chase Country Club and have them change my membership to 'out-of-town.'"

Tubman's Funeral in Liberia

Liberia may be a mess today, like most of West Africa, but at the time of President Tubman's funeral, it was a lively and interesting place, albeit a very self-conscious and formal one. In any event, I got to go to the funeral. Official Washington was particularly interested in Liberia because so many of the ruling elite attended college in America, and at Howard University in particular.

For those who don't know, Liberia was created by President James Monroe as part of a program to do something about slavery in the early nineteenth century—but without abolishing slavery. The idea was to get rid of slavery gradually by freeing slaves and sending them to Africa, specifically Liberia. The Abolition Society managed to purchase the much larger area that was then Liberia and arranged to send freed slaves there.

As President Monroe was a prominent proponent of this concept, the capital city is named Monrovia. Even Abraham Lincoln supported the program before the Civil War and wondered if the Federal government could raise enough money to buy all of the slaves in America and send them "back to Africa."

The U.S. bought Liberia from the native tribes, and a number of former slaves did indeed return to their roots, although most African Americans preferred to stay in America. Over time, the neighboring countries took away parts of the original territory by war. But enough remained. The approximately 25,000 former slaves from America became the ruling class, some even, in turn, making slaves of the native Blacks in the interior. This 25,000 ruling class were called the "Amerigos." Descendants from this group formed the ruling class, and they lived a privileged existence.

They spoke English, went to American schools and colleges, and created a government copied word for word from our original Constitution (though unamended). They had states—one named Maryland, for instance—and they had a president and vice president, House, Senate, Cabinet and court system with a Supreme Court.

William Vanarat Tubman had been chief justice of the Supreme Court before he was elected president. While on the Supreme Court, Tubman was touched by scandal for keeping slaves on his rubber plantation. Tubman's death in 1971 created a constitutional issue never faced in our own country. He was the sitting president, and had been reelected, however he died after the election but before his inauguration. The question was who succeeded him. Was it to be the vice president, a Baptist minister and president of the

World Baptist Alliance named Taylor, also a friend of my good friend Jerry Moore, also a Baptist minister and vice president himself of the World Baptist Alliance? Or was the acting secretary of state to be the successor? The matter was decided in their Supreme Court, and Taylor became president and was later inaugurated.

Rubber was king in Liberia. The great rubber companies in America took their whole crop and set up thousands of acres of rubber trees. The companies curried favor with the wealthy and politically influential by doling out plots to the politicians and officials, who thereby became wealthy.

Bob Finch, former lieutenant governor of California and our friend (Mrs. Finch and Margot created Clothing for Children, providing public school students who had no school clothes with used and cleaned clothes donated to the cause) named me to part of the delegation. Bob Finch started out as secretary of HEW, but was relieved of the job by his friend Richard Nixon when he almost had a nervous breakdown (probably caused by Nixon!) and became a presidential counselor. The president appointed Finch to be head of the delegation to the funeral, and Finch, in turn appointed about twenty of us to go along.

The Liberians were not happy with Finch. If they could not have Nixon at the funeral, they wanted the vice president, Mr. Agnew, who by chance had been in Africa at the time of Tubman's death. The Liberians were offended that Americans did not take this occasion seriously enough. Liberia considered itself our best friend in Africa and felt that more respect should have been paid. What made matters worse was that *Time* magazine (which "they" all read, meaning the Amerigos) called Tubman "the father of the country," but the context made it clear that this meant that he had reportedly sired 100 bastard children in his time.

Our party left Andrews Airport on Air Force 2, and in what seemed like no time, we put down at the Monrovia Airport.

We had been directed to bring with us:

1) White Tie and Tails
2) Black Tie
3) Morning Clothes and Top Hat, and
4) Business Suit with White Shirt and Four-in-Hand Tie

Liberia was formal, and at one occasion or another we wore all of these outfits. At the religious services, for instance, we wore white tie and tails. The services involved a Baptist minister, a red-headed Irish Catholic priest, and a Muslim imam. At the graveside service, we wore morning clothes and top hat. It was always beastly hot, but our delegation endured, to a man and woman (in black dresses and black stockings).

In contrast to Liberia's strict formality, there was the prime minister from Ghana, wearing a loin cloth with one strap over his bare shoulders. Despite his much cooler attire, he keeled over in the heat, but we did not.

The guest list included a crossroads of Africa and the rest of the whole wide world. Emperor Haile Selassie was there in his British brigadier general's uniform. General Gowan, the ruler of Nigeria, was there, as was the speaker of the Knesset in Israel and one of Queen Elizabeth's sons (not the Prince of Wales, however). The speaker of the Knesset was of interest because Israel was then riding high in Africa and had all their votes in the U.N. (alas, this is no longer the case). The reason for this was that Israel was furnishing intelligence services to all African countries and teaching their leaders, including General Gowan, how to fly military planes.

From the formal dress and punctilious ceremony, the funeral descended into comic opera. The Liberians had obviously taken note of President Kennedy's funeral with the black riderless horse, the empty saddle, and the boots reversed in the stirrups. As no horse could survive the Liberian climate, they got a weapons carrier, put a saddle on it, and had the boots reversed in the stirrups.

The Liberian air force—two Piper Cubs and a DC-3—flew over the ceremony. The navy consisted of one motor yacht used by the president for pleasure. The army, in the form of an augmented squad, attended. When parade rest was ordered, the privates laid their rifles in the dirt.

The American ambassador was a history professor on leave from Howard University, and Mayor Walter Washington had asked the ambassador's lovely wife to look out for me. She took me in hand, warning me never in this climate to eat the deviled eggs at the first night's buffet. She saved my life.

On the way to one party, however, I thought I would lose my life. I was walking from my apartment to the party, when I found myself surrounded by "savages." They wore grass skirts, were naked from the waist up, and carried huge machetes. They formed a ring around me, crowded in and raised their machetes. Slowly, it dawned on me: they were having fun with me.

During Tubman's tenure as president, he had shown concern for the welfare of the "natives." As a result, they were saddened by his death, and came into Monrovia from the jungle to be nearby when he was buried. The group I encountered were obviously drunk, and were making an "Irish Wake" of the funeral.

Later on, there was a disastrous revolution in Liberia led by "Sergeant Doe." Vice President Taylor and all the young Amerigos I had met were all killed, and the country returned to anarchy and the jungle. Thus, in a way, I was present at the Liberian "Camelot."

We Get to Go to the White House

As I said in an earlier story, one of the distinct pleasures of being a City Council chairman and hence a City Father was getting to go to the White House. Among the best events were the formal receptions and dinners at the White House, the only place in the world where the officeholder goes through the receiving line ahead of his spouse. Margot always hated this because the president would greet me, and then say to Mrs. Nixon, "You remember Gilbert Hahn, who is our chairman of the City Council." Then he would look at Margot and say, "This is ... unh ..." Margot always threatened to say, "Fuck you, Mr. President," and I sometimes thought she would, so powerful was her dislike for Richard Nixon.

But even Margot had to admit that the morning ceremonies greeting the kings, presidents, and prime ministers on official visits to the White House always made for a marvelous outing. There would always be one of the ceremonial units drawn up, and the visiting dignitary's entourage, ambassadors, state department officials, and a few of us representing the city and the Federal government would be lined up in our appointed places' for the ceremony. Afterwards, coffee and orange juice was served. A chance to shake hands with and meet the great and powerful for a few minutes would always be followed by dining-out stories.

Once, after the special visit by the French president, the State Department gave a luncheon in the State Department dining room and served American wines! The French were lavish in their praise of the wines. Margot stuck one of the menus listing all the wines from California into her pocketbook and later asked our local wine merchant to try to get us some. To our surprise we were told that these wines were unobtainable outside of California—except as in this case for the luncheon for the French.

*   *   *   *   *

On another occasion, Margot made the interesting observation that Indira Ghandi didn't shave her legs.

ERRATA SHEET

Page 63

The subheading should read "I. W. Bernheim and Schmieheim." In three places on page 63 the name "Burnham" is a typographical error and should read "Bernheim." However, the company name, "I. W. Burnham & Co.," is correct.

Page 64

The name "Burnham" is a typographical error and should read "Bernheim."

Page 68

The name "Burnham" is a typographical error and should read "Bernheim."

*   *   *   *   *

During the memorable visit of Israel Prime Minister Golda Meir to Washington, the Israel ambassador, Itzhak Rabin, gave a reception for Mrs. Meir. Margot and I were standing around when we noticed Mrs. Meir, apparently by herself. We went over to talk to her.

Margot and I had admired Mrs. Meir that morning, wearing her ground-gripper shoes and holding her huge handbag, with her gray hair tied in a severe bun behind her head, marching alongside Mr. Nixon reviewing the troops.

Margot said, "Mrs. Meir, as a woman, I wanted to tell you how proud I was to see the way you reviewed the troops."

Mrs. Meir replied, "Honey, was I all right?"

I. W. Burnham and Schmieheim

Margot's great grandfather I. W. (Isaac Wolf Burnham) was quite a guy. Born in a small German village called Schmieheim on the Alsace-Lorraine border close to Baden-Baden, he came to America before the Civil War and started out as an itinerant peddler with a horse and wagon selling "pins and notions" at farm houses in the Midwest.

When he got to Paducah, Kentucky, his horse died, so he planted his roots.

He and a Negro helper made I. W. Harper, a bourbon whisky that became a great success. From that beginning, he went on to become a multimillionaire, eventually owning Babo cleanser, I. W. Burnham & Co., and the Pittsburgh Pirates. (He had brought a relative, Barney Dreyfuss, from Germany. Unfortunately, Barney was of little help in the distillery as he was sickly, so I. W. bought the Pittsburgh Pirates so Barney could have an "out-of-doors work.") Years later, to the shock of family and friends, I. W. Burnham, blinded by cataracts, fell off his terrace in California. To their even greater shock, it turned out he had left all his money to found the vast Burnham Forrest outside Louisville as a place that people who couldn't afford membership in country clubs could enjoy.

In his memoirs, which he paid to have published, great grandfather Burnham explained how he returned rich and famous to Schmieheim, his native village, stopping first at Baden-Baden. He was greeted at the station by Herr Brenner, owner of Brenner's Park Hotel in Baden-Baden. Burnham's return to Schmieheim was, of course, triumphant, especially after he offered to restore the local castle (*Schloss*) as a gift to the town.

If it was all the same to him, said the townspeople, they would rather have running water for the village, so he did as asked, paying for it to be done.

In the 1980s, Margot and the children and I took a trip to Alsace and visited Strasbourg, the location of the parliament of Europe, and dined at as many of the famous restaurants (of which there are many delectable examples) as the days allowed. When we left Strasbourg to stay at Brenner Park Hotel ourselves, Margot suddenly said, "Let's go to Schmieheim."

It was not even on the map, nor was there even a road sign warning of its approach, at least not until we'd almost passed it, but our guide and driver was lucky, and we stumbled upon the village. I was sitting in front with the driver when we saw it. "It" looked to be a horse trough with a stanchion and spigot for water. On the trough were the words "Burnham Brunen."

I called out, "Stop the car!" And there it was: "Burnham fountain" right on the main (and only) street of the village. I saw the only modern building, a one-man branch bank of a huge German national bank. I went in to make inquiries about the fountain.

As a child I had had a German nurse, and as a result I spoke some German, though not for forty years. Nonetheless I tried.

"Mein Frau ist ein Burnham."

I was taken aback by the reply! "Juden?" ("Jewish")

Thinking he meant me, I said "Ja." And he motioned me to wait and be patient while he sent a boy, who was apparently sitting there for just that purpose, off on his bicycle to get the village schoolmaster and oral historian. While we waited, I communicated as best I could in my halting German, and learned that the clerk/teller, far from meaning to insult me, had said what he did only to be sure that we were talking about the famous Jew Burnham, the patron of Schmieheim. This was explained to us in full detail when the oral historian arrived. He told us all about their gratitude to Margot's ancestor, and made us feel welcome in Schmieheim.

Schmieheim was too tiny for an inn, bistro, or bar, so we were entertained in the oral historian's home. He pointed out the former synagogue had been turned into a bicycle factory. "Did we wish to visit the Jewish Cemetery?" "No." "What else could they do for us?" "Nothing thanks," but it wasn't important. What was important was that Margot had found her "roots."

Martin Agronsky

I first met Martin in 1948 when I returned to Washington as a young lawyer just starting out in practice. Martin had a news program on WOL, the Mutual Broadcasting System's Washington station. His sponsor was my father, the head of our family's retail shoe business. Perhaps that was why Martin was so nice to me. But whatever the case, a real friendship developed. Martin and his (first) wife Helen kept a "salon" featuring spaghetti dinners with newsworthy people in the nation's capital, and though not at all newsworthy myself, I became a regular guest.

Martin was the first famous war correspondent I had ever met (also the *only* one, come to think of it!), but I had heard him most evenings on my radio in college at Princeton. Before the United States entered World War II, Martin was one of a well-known team of correspondents that CBS kept in London, Paris, and Berlin. Martin was on the roundup each evening with: "This is Martin Agronsky in Ankara, Turkey."

One night Martin was reporting on an unfair, one-sided trade agreement involving acorns that had been forced on Turkey by the Germans. Germany, in the person of Ambassador Von Pappen, did not care to have the agreement described as Germany "bullying" Turkey. Nevertheless, Martin, in discussing the deal, ended with, "You know, acorns; that's nuts." Von Pappen, who understood the American idiom, pressured Turkish officials to throw Martin out of the country, and they did so.

According to his version of events, Agronsky left Ankara, heading East, to get back to America and arrived in China in December 1941, the time of the bombing of Pearl Harbor. He said that the first ship he took for home was sunk by the Japanese. He also said that he was rescued by a second ship that was headed for Australia, but that the Japanese also sank that ship, and he finally made it to Australia in a lifeboat. In any case, I believed him.

According to Martin's account, he slept the first night ashore in an inn on the beach, and then he went out early the next morning for a swim. (He was a great ocean swimmer from his early life in Atlantic City.) When he came back to the inn with his hair wet, the innkeeper asked where he had been. "Swimming in the ocean," he said. The innkeeper turned pale and said, "That area is the world's most shark infested waters. No one swims there!" That was Martin.

In Australia, Martin met Helen, an army nurse, and married her. She was a lovely person who was always kind to Margot and me.

In the 1950s, Martin got a television program on NBC that was intended to compete with Edward R. Murrow's "I Can See It Now." His first show, very splashy, was an hour interview with John Foster Dulles, Eisenhower's secretary of state. One of the next programs was an hour interview with the famous author Bud Schulberg (*On the Waterfront, What Makes Sammy Run*, etc.). The interview was about this new movie about the Everglades, which starred Burl Ives.

Because of the Florida Everglades theme, the program was held at a Florida resort in Boca Raton (far from the Everglades). The setting was a houseboat on a neighboring creek. As Margot and I were visiting my parents in Miami Beach, Martin and Helen invited us to come to Boca Raton to watch the show live, which was how most shows were done in the early days of television.

The show wandered about, from the movie to both Schulberg's and Ives' flirtation with the Communist Party, and then to Schulberg's working in the beet fields to help a supposedly Communist labor union organize the agricultural workers in California. Then it got to the subject of Thomas Heggen, who had written *Mr. Roberts*. His book had been a huge bestseller, a smash play on Broadway, and a box-office success as a movie. Despite, or perhaps because of, all this success, Thomas Heggen had developed writer's block and was afraid to write his second book, let it fail, and then write the third, fourth, and so on. Heggen, it turned out, had committed suicide over his depression, and Schulberg held himself responsible, believing he should have persuaded him against it.

At first, it was an interesting exchange, but Schulberg and Martin got stuck on this subject, like a broken record, and never got off it. Because the show was live, this went on and on and didn't stop until the program ended. Then, as if to top this sad story, Martin got a call from New York. His producer (and patron) had just dropped dead—Martin's show was canceled on the spot.

Martin and Bud drove back to Miami, with Margot in the front seat between them (this pre-dated the days of bucket seats). I drove Helen back in my car, and we arrived at a drunken "wake." Martin and Bud had gotten roaring drunk over the end of the program and the failed show. Margot thought they would surely crack up on the way, and we were both pleased when she arrived safely.

Danny and Betty Angel

My friend of fifty years Danny Angel died the other day, and his wife Betty two days later. The Angels lived in London where he was a famous movie producer in England. Margot and I first met Danny and Betty on the beach at Deauville in 1950, on our honeymoon to France.

We had been staying at an inexpensive hotel on the Left Bank that had an Air Algiers counter in the lobby. Our room was opposite an airshaft, and I well remember the somber cat at the other end of the airshaft who watched us all night long through the window. Even though we had very little money, the hotel rates were so inexpensive that we were able to keep our room, rent a small Peugeot, ride into eastern France, and visit the scenes of my World War II sites at Epernay, Rheims, Metz, and a town then named "Bourg" where I was wounded while on a forward observer mission in the final attack on Metz late in November 1944.

We climbed up on one of the slag heaps that cover eastern France and viewed the scene of my near demise. After that, we went on to Deauville for a day's visit and stayed in Trouville next door, pretending we were staying in Deauville.

During the War, I had spent some months in the U.S. Army Hospital at St. Albans in England. It got the "overs" (artillery speak for rounds that overshoot the target) from London from the V-1s and the V-2s. But, as it was also just a short train ride from London, I went as frequently as I was allowed out of the hospital. The first time there, I went to the Windmill Theater, owned and operated by an impresario with the wonderful name of Vivian Van Damme. Just off Picadilly Circus on Great Windmill Street, it is the English version of the American burlesque house. All the great comedians, such as Sydney Fields, got their starts there. They had the great beauties of the day posing as nudes. Unfortunately, the lord chamberlin, the moral guru of the English stage, would only allow them to do so in "tableau," meaning they had to pose stationary, or the theater got closed.

At the beach on that day in Deauville, we heard the bar attendant address the father of the group on the next blanket as Mister Van Damme. I was sure it was he when I saw that Mr. Van Damme was dressed in pink pants, the first man I had ever seen so attired. Mr. Van Damme was surrounded by his wife, his daughter, his son-in-law, and a pilot for his private airplane.

We became friends. Van Damme took Margot under his wing—taught her how to play Trent et Quarant ("30 and 40"). And each night she won enough for us to stay one more day. Finally, we had to go back to Paris.

The daughter Betty and the son-in-law Daniel were our friends for fifty years thereafter, visiting us both in Washington and on the Eastern Shore.

Danny was the son of the family that owned Angels, a costume and fancy-dress firm (like Moss Brothers, which was pronounced "Moss Bross"), but Danny didn't want the family business. World War II came, and Danny was aboard a troop ship in the Norway debacle, and then a trooper in India where he caught polio so that for the rest of his life he had to be on crutches and later in a wheelchair. But this did not stop him from becoming a massive success in the movie business. He had many famous films like *Murder at the Windmill* (about his father-in-law's theater) and *Reach for the Stars*, about a famous RAF pilot , Douglas Bader, who lost his legs yet returned to fight in the air.

Danny always thought I was an expert on American politics, and so we spent hours going over its ins-and-outs. The last time we were in London, we missed Danny, but we said we would get him the next time. We didn't, and he died the other day. We truly loved Danny and Betty.

A Compliment to Treasure

In the year 2000, I had a heart attack, but it had a happy ending. In all honesty, I have only myself to blame for the heart attack. Looking back on my eating habits over the years, and in light of what I now know about what constitutes a proper diet, I am horrified at the thought of what I have stuffed into my stomach.

A series of chest pains over an eighteen-month period culminated in an ambulance ride to Johns Hopkins Hospital in Baltimore and a quadruple by-pass operation. As I was out of commission, Margot had to struggle with decisions on my behalf. Unfortunately, her temporary indecision about contacting the doctor we wanted to do the operation, Dr. Levi Watkins, an extraordinarily gifted African-American surgeon and the head of Hopkins' cardiac department, gave Dr. Watkins the wrong impression, and, when finally asked, he declined. (Considering that Margot's grandfather Bertram Burnham, a famous vascular surgeon, was denied a full professorship at Hopkins because he was a Jew, the fact that Dr. Watkins was department head is an indication that times do indeed change.)

As it happens, Margot and I have a dear friend at Howard University Hospital, Dr. LaSalle LaFall, a famous cancer expert who is also African American. Figuring, correctly, that Drs. Watkins and LaFall were probably friends, Margot asked Dr. LaFall to intercede for us with Dr. Watkins and ask him to change his mind and operate on me. Dr. LaFall did so, and Dr. Watkins agreed.

After it was all over, Dr. Watkins told me what Dr. LaFall had said that caused him to change his mind. He said Dr. LaFall had told him about my service to the city of Washington, D.C., and its community over the years. He said that in referring to me, LaSalle LaFall had used the word "blessed."

Even though I didn't know exactly what this meant, I certainly knew what it implied, and I have said ever since that it was the most extravagant compliment ever paid to me. In fact, it was almost worth having the heart attack.

University Terrace

Margot and I built our home at University Terrace in Northwest Washington on land that was supposed to have been sold to a church. Our University Terrace neighbor, Judge David Bazelon, who was famous for his liberal opinions, especially that of the *Durham* case, which established insanity as a defense against criminal charges, urged us to buy the land so that a church would not go next door to his home. We did. Both Margot and I were fond of David and his wife, Mickie, and we had him as our guest during one terrific five-day snow storm.

Our wonderful one-level, all glass and flagstone house was designed by David Yerkes and features a stark and plain yet colorful interior design by Ed Benesch, and landscaping by Tommy Church from California. So important to the development and appearance of the house was the blend of interior and exterior work that the architects, annoyed by the interference and overpowering of their building, refused to continue supervising the construction. So Margot had to come over, every day, brown bag in hand, to supervise it herself.

The only thing we ever had to complain about is winter weather. Snow and ice play havoc with our steeply slopping entrance, making it all but impossible to get in or out under those conditions. On our first snow, while I was City Council chairman, a city snow removal crew, no doubt seeking to please me, cleared University Terrace before any other street in Washington.

Knowing how items like this can backfire if they make the pages of the *Washington Post* or the *Star*, I called the Department of Public Works and said, "Don't ever do that again," by which I meant, of course, don't clear my street before others. Unfortunately, the department took me literally, and from that day to this they have never cleared snow from University Terrace at all, to the sorrow and dismay of our neighbors.

A Barge Trip to Melun

Margot and I have made frequent trips to Paris, especially to stay at the Ritz Hotel. It is one of our most cherished experiences, each time, and it never gets old. But one year, Margot said, "Instead of staying in Paris, let's take a barge trip." So we arranged to take a barge trip that was leaving Paris from one of the quais. What we didn't know was that all of the other passengers were fast friends and we would be the only outsiders.

With our passage paid for, there was nothing to do but have a car from the Ritz drop us off at the quai. Once aboard, we got our cabin, with its combination toilet and shower stall, and made the best of it. Lunch was served as we headed down the Seine.

I was particularly interested in our first stop, Melun. In September of 1944, as an artillery forward observer and fire direction center commander, I had crossed the Seine at Melun as part of the Third Army's "rat race" that took place across France in the waning summer and fall of that year. (Today there is a plaque memorializing that passage of the Third Army across France and into Germany.) But when we got to Melun, the pleasure of the unexpected visit was rudely interrupted.

Just as we arrived, so did the Duane, the French tax collectors, in a fleet of cars to arrest the barge and its operators! We sat for hours while secret talks took place between the Duane and the boat owners. The owners and operators, who were Canadian, were being charged with not having paid taxes to France, but it later turned out that the whole thing was a mistake and they did not owe anything. The Canadians' *real* crime was that they were not French. So, instead of putting a lien on the boat, as would have happened in America, and thus allowing the barge to finish its trip, the Duane required the *bargistes* to return to Paris.

The group of friends on the boat were terrified and remained on board, but Margot and I got off. We managed to place a call to our friend David Campbell, the manager of the Ritz. "Go to the railroad station at Melun," he said, "and we'll send a limo and driver to pick you up." The limo arrived, faithfully, and drove us at breakneck speed through the lovely French evening back to the Ritz where we were regally installed—in the Duke and Duchess of Windsor's suite—for the night.

Later, the barge owners came to see us, said the entire tax matter was a misunderstanding, and refunded our passage. Consequently, we (still) love Paris in the fall.

Clayton Fritchey

My friend Clayton Fritchey died in February 2001. His obituary said he was 96, but my guess is that he was over 100.

A large cocktail party was held in his honor at the home where he and wife Polly had lived for many years. Margot and I had been their friends for a very long time and had enjoyed dinners at both their home in Georgetown and their great farm on the Eastern Shore near Galena, Maryland. We'd played innumerable games of bridge with them, even though the games often broke up with Clayton shouting at Polly and driving her to tears.

The memorials at the cocktail party were given by Arnold Sagalyn—who'd known Clayton when Clayton edited the *Cleveland Press* and introduced Arnold to Elliot Ness, then cleaning up crime and corruption in Cleveland, as chronicled by Clayton—Senator Gaylord Nelson, Ambassador Frank Wisner, Polly's son, and Kay Graham.

Clayton had worked on papers in Baltimore and New Orleans in addition to Cleveland, had served General Marshall as his press secretary, and then Adlai Stevenson, in both his presidential campaign and at the U.N. He'd had a long and interesting career, spiced by his many love affairs with beautiful women—all of whom had beautiful legs—during his bachelor days. An elegant conversationalist and a superb dancer, he was, as implied above, a great ladies man.

I got to know Clayton when my law partner Bruce Sundlund, later governor of Rhode Island, my friend Bernie Bralove, owner of the Shoreham Hotel, and I joined forces to buy a printing plant in Georgetown. After we'd acquired the plant, Bernie opined that to make a go of it we needed a newspaper. At the time, the *Alexandria Gazette*, a storied daily with a long and mostly successful history, owned another paper, the *Arlington Sun*, that was a money-loser, and the directors of the company had ordered the *Gazette* to sell the *Sun*. We were in the process of trying to buy the Arlington paper when Clayton Fritchey appeared on the scene. He said that he and three of his friends were interested in publishing a suburban daily in the Northern Virginia area to be modeled on Long Island's *Newsday*, a suburban tabloid-style paper that competed with the New York dailies outside of New York. Would we like to become partners with them? We would, and we did. Clayton's trio of friends were the aforementioned Arnold Sagalyn, George Ball, who would later become an assistant secretary of state, and Sears-Roebuck family scion Phil Stern.

They put up a lot of money, produced the paper, and eventually bought out Sundlun, Bralove, and Hahn. But Sundlun and I remained in the picture, as, in the early days—which were truly days of trial and tribulation for the paper—we did a lot of legal work for them and helped with labor problems. In order to compete with the established papers, they tried to run a non-union paper (or a union paper with relaxed rules), which caused any number of problems, in addition to their legal ones, such as threats and acts of sabotage like putting sugar in the gas tanks of their trucks.

The principal union involved, the International Typesetters Union, or ITU, was warned by the *Washington Post* that whatever concessions they might make to the *Sun* would also have to be given to the *Post*. Similar problems arose with advertisers, with major advertisers being warned that if they advertised in the *Sun* they could forget about advertising space in the *Post*. But Editor-in-Chief Clayton Fritchey and his staff soldiered on.

Before it was all over, I had a moment in the sun, but it was journalistic rather than legal. While all this was going on, Margot and I made a trip on the *Queen Mary* to England, and when I learned that John Wayne and his wife, Pilar, were on board, I thought I'd request an interview. To my surprise, over cocktails with our wives, Wayne accepted. I did the interview, wrote it up, and the *Sun* printed it. (I have never forgotten Pilar. A gorgeous lady, she also had the most beautiful feet I have ever seen on a woman, except for my own wife, and the most beautiful shoes on those feet. Yes, that's possible.)

Also in their party was the director of Wayne's most recent films, John Huston. As the vessel neared England, it did not put in to the nearest port for us to disembark. Instead, great tenders came out to it, and passengers and baggage were loaded onto them. Because of the presence on board of John Wayne and Huston, the press came out to meet and interview them. At one point, Huston was asked what he was going to do next. Before he answered, he propped my wife up on a railing, fixed the hem of her dress just above her knees, and said, "I'm going to make this young lady a movie star."

Josh Miner

Josh Miner and I go way back. Classmates at Exeter where we both played football, we went on to Princeton together and remained close friends. Both of us joined the field artillery ROTC. Leaving Princeton in 1942, instead of '43, we went to Officer Candidate School in Fort Sill, Oklahoma, where we were commissioned as lieutenants in the field artillery, Josh in self-propelled 105s and I in self-propelled 155s.

After the War, Josh went to the field of molding boys in secondary schools, his first assignment being the renowned Gordonstone School in England—which included students such as Prince Philip—where the headmaster was the famous Kurt Hahn (not, I'm afraid, a relative). Kurt Hahn was legendary for his sense of fairness. Once, after a track meet, when Hahn learned that the athletes from the opposing school had been competing without shoes, he made his Gordonstone boys take off theirs and start the meet all over.

In World War II, Kurt Hahn had founded Outward Bound to help teach the sailors of the British Merchant Marine how to survive in lifeboats after being torpedoed by German subs. Following Hahn's lead, when Josh returned to the United States he founded Outward Bound in this country to teach character traits as well as survival skills to American boys and girls of all ages in activities like mountaineering and white water rafting all over the world.

Back in America, Josh joined the faculty at Andover, and never left. Also a legend in his own time, he became not just admissions counselor, but Andover's own "Mr. Chips." While there, he oversaw the admission and education of not one but two American presidents named George Bush.

Bright, effervescent, and always interested in all of his old friends, Josh also became famous in the world of college admissions by writing the nicest and wittiest letters to college admissions officers all over the United States to get our children admitted into college. Whenever he came to Washington, or Meetinghouse Cove on the Eastern Shore, it was always an event.

Last year Billy Sloan, our mutual friend and former classmate at both Exeter and Princeton and also a fellow field artillery lieutenant, called to tell me Josh had incurable cancer, and while he was not taking any treatment, he did want to hear from his old friend Gil. Knowing that crying wouldn't help, I called instead. Before I could tell him how sorry I was, he said, with all of his old forcefulness, "I'm a fraud. I don't feel anything."

I wish I had his guts.

Chapter 5

ೞ)ೞ

World War II

War Stories, 1942–1946

My father had the good sense in 1941 to urge me to join the Field Artillery ROTC at Princeton so that when the war broke out I was able to look forward to going in as a second lieutenant in the actual field artillery. I went from Princeton into the army in 1942, was given sergeant's stripes at Camp Meade, and was shipped to Fort Sill to the Officers Candidate School. Fort Sill, the premier hotbed of field artillery training in World War II, was an interesting place. It was such an old army post that *Geronimo* had been kept a prisoner there.

During the Officers Candidate School course at Fort Sill, I began to see for the first time what the rest of the country was all about. Because of a mix-up in my medical records, I was not at Fort Sill along with my Princeton classmates, but with a grab bag of all kinds of young men from different backgrounds from all over the country.

The one I remember best (but whose name I have forgotten) had been a policeman in Richmond, Virginia. Once he learned I was a graduate of Princeton, he used to tell stories just for my benefit. And he used to tell silly, dirty stories in which the participants were always the Yale Man and the "Hartford" [sic] Man.

I'd already had an extensive artillery background during ROTC, and as a result I became very popular as a coach to the other candidates for commission by helping them with gunnery, surveying, and the mathematics of it all. After I received my commission, I was sent to Camp Roberts, California, but before reporting there I got a leave to come home to Washington.

The popular thing to do in those days was to go out to the nearest army airfield and cadge rides on the army planes to wherever we were going. The price was right—zero—but we rarely got a direct flight. For example, on that occasion I got a ride from Tulsa, Oklahoma, to Wright Field in Dayton, Ohio. When I went out to get on the second plane at Wright Field, the one going from Dayton to Washington, D.C., I was so dumb that I nearly walked into the propeller. I couldn't see it, and it almost ended my career, and life, right then and there. To get back to Camp Roberts, I took the overnight train from Washington to Chicago, and then the Super Chief from Chicago to Los Angeles. (I no longer remember how I got from Los Angeles to Camp Roberts.)

Camp Roberts was a relatively new army post about half-way between Los Angeles and San Francisco; it was located near William Randolph Hearst's San Simeon Ranch, a large part of which became the Hunter-Ligget military reservation where we did our gunnery training with sand-filled shells. The men liked to go out with their carbines and shoot the deer that ran wild on the ranch. During Hearst's time, the ranch was filled with exotic animals such as giraffes. However, all the exotic animals had been scooped up and sent to zoos, and only the red deer remained.

The 558th Field Artillery Battalion was made up from a cadre out of a Colorado National Guard Artillery Regiment. In those days, cadres were fitted out with the least-promising officers and the biggest screw-ups in the noncommissioned ranks, and ours was no exception. We started with such an overload of losers that the army sent in a group of bright, young, and green second lieutenants to help with the training. The "fillers" were young high school kids from the American northwest, mostly Utah, and among other interesting people were American Indians and one cashiered navy officer, a graduate of the U.S. Naval Academy. This bumptious and unpromising group, which started from zero, was trained so well that nine months later we hit the beaches at Utah Beach in Normandy and became part of General Patton's Third Army (and served as corps artillery to the XIIth and XXth Corps).

What we got for weapons was something comparatively new, but still made up of hand-me-down equipment. These were the battalions' twelve guns and twelve ammunition carriers. The guns were made up of French 155 guns—that's a six-inch barrel that could fire from twenty thousand meters, but the gun barrels were old French 155 guns, so-called 155 GPF (Grand Puissance), left over from World War I mounted on the lower part of old M-3 tanks. That was the brand new part—having heavy artillery self-propelled. That is, they were propelled by the tank tracks that carried them, rather than being drawn by horses or trucks.

Most of the senior officers in the battalion turned out to be very unsatisfactory. Colonel Conway was an otherwise lovely man who got replaced in combat. Major Thorne was my immediate boss as the S-3, that is, he was in charge of operations or fire control, and I was the assistant S-3 in charge of the fire direction center. Major Thorne was killed, the other major was cashiered for cowardice, and a number of the officers got sent home or the next thing to it.

The wonder is that we managed to march and shoot credibly throughout the war. I don't know what would have happened to us had we suffered any reverses on the battlefield; but fortunately nothing ever happened. We landed a few days after the invasion on Utah Beach, in time to take part in the breakout by the Third Army from Normandy, and wound up south of Paris before it fell (in July and August), occupying a position south of Orleans. There we provided infantry support for a band of French Marquis who were commanded by a tall De Gaulle look-a-like with a nom de guerre of "Colonel O'Neill."

For years, I always thought this story about Colonel O'Neill improbable, until looking at the battalion history, which I had been assigned to write after the war was over, I saw there in the records of the battalion the name *Colonel O'Neill* and the place *Orleans*.

The events at Orleans: The Ninth Army had invaded the south of France at Saint Tropez and were pushing to the north the Germans who were trying to get to Paris (which had not yet fallen) to escape; we and the French Marquis were either shooting at them or accepting the surrender of thousands of Germans caught between ourselves and the Ninth Army as it began its great performance. The Third Army, in crossing the Seine at Melun, became engaged in what we called the "rat race." We went from Orleans to Metz, or the outskirts of it, in about four to six weeks, with nothing but cold rations, oil and gasoline, relatively little food, and no ammunition. What we did basically was to pound on through Epernay, Rheims, and then into the outskirts of Metz, where I stood in the town square on my birthday, September 12, with not a German in sight. Behind me, all the way back to Rheims, was the Third Army, stranded and out of gasoline.

What happened next was a meeting (well described in the book *A Bridge Too Far*) in which gasoline was given to Montgomery in the fateful disaster called Market Garden and the failure to cross the bridge at the River Rhine, while the Third Army sat for forty-five days in the Saar-Moselle Triangle. I spent those forty-five days as a forward observer on the hills overlooking the Saar-Moselle Valley, spotting to shoot at German field artillery.

All of this German field artillery was horse-drawn (I am able to astonish all my friends even to this day by telling them that my subsequent investigation found that almost the entire German army was horse-drawn, not mechanized as is the popular fancy). The horse-drawn field artillery were very good though and gave us a tough time, dashing into position and firing off a few rounds very accurately, hitching up the horses to the guns, and pulling out almost before we could zero in on them.

We stayed outside of Metz for this forty-five-day period. During that time, some of my pals, the other lieutenants in the battalion, took their guns for direct lay missions on the various forts around Metz. My friend Bryce Bowmar, in an heroic episode, fired into those forts at one thousand yards. (He is mentioned in Stephen Ambrose's book *Citizen Soldier*.) My other friend who did the same thing, Brandon Bodell, was killed.

The concept of the direct lay missions was not ideal, because with separate loading ammunition, a shell from a machine gun or mortar could explode the powder bag (that had to be kept at the gun), so it was highly dangerous.

Along about Thanksgiving, we began a new attack on Metz. I went ahead as a forward observer with the infantry and was wounded by shell fragments from a mortar shell in a town then appearing on the map as Bourg, which is simply the German name for *city*. (Margot and I were not able to locate the town on our visit to the battlefield in 1950.)

I spent a good number of months in the hospitals in eastern France, Paris, and finally in St. Albans in England, and had a number of operations followed by steady recovery. During that period, I got to visit London from time to time—and came nearer to being killed by V1s and V2s than I ever had in France.

I should say a word or two about General Patton. I always felt grateful for my life to George S. Patton. Anyone who has seen the movie about his life will, I am sure, remember the opening scene where he talks to the audience of soldiers. What he had to say in that scene was from a collection of speeches he made to junior officers before the invasion, and I was present at one of them. I heard him use the line "No son of a bitch ever won a war by dying for his country. You win a war by getting the other son of a bitch to die for *his* country." Then he talked to us about how we had to go forward, keep moving forward, never stop, and that more of us would come home alive. Thankfully, this turned out to be true.

It was amazing how he did things that made us feel that he had his hand on us. We were never allowed to go around without our helmets on, or without wearing neckties, even in the dead of winter and in combat. He managed to instill a fear in us so that we were more afraid of him, General Patton, than we were of the Germans. And it worked! We *were* more afraid of him than the Germans. It was as simple as that.

You didn't dare be given a mission and say, "I wouldn't" or "I couldn't," because that's how leadership worked. Another measure of how well it worked was that the Third Army's percentage of casualties was considerably lower than, say, that of the First Army commanded by General Bradley, who was supposed to be the GI's best friend. The GI's best friend was definitely George Patton.

He came upon me one day while I was doing my stint as forward observer from a revetment on the hills overlooking the Saar-Moselle Valley and upbraided me for doing what we all did, which was to cover the insignia on the front of our helmets with mud so that snipers wouldn't sight in on us.

Patton said, "Lieutenant, are you afraid of the Germans?" I lied and said, "No Sir, General Patton." And he said, "Well then get that mud off your helmet," and dashed off in his command car with all of the blaring horns and painted stars.

I was terrified that his exposure at my hill observation post would attract so much attention from the German artillery that he might be killed there. (I hoped it wouldn't happen at *my* observation post!) You always felt when you were serving under his command that he was making the best possible use of you, and thus winning the war.

When I was released from the hospital and got back to my battalion in May 1945, I found it combat-loaded in Marseille ready to leave for Japan to land on one of the Japanese islands where our self-propelled 155s would be used for direct lay missions against the Japanese in their caves. I had just survived the war in France and Germany, but I had a sinking feeling that I might not survive the second part of the war, the part in Japan.

We were loaded into a troop ship, and as we passed Gibraltar and headed for the Panama Canal, we heard over the radio that the first bomb had been dropped on Hiroshima. As we got to the South Atlantic and closer to the Panama Canal, the second bomb was dropped on Nagasaki. The war ended, and the ship turned around and headed for Jersey City and home. Since I attribute the dropping of the bomb to removing me from danger on the Japanese shores, I conclude that I have always loved the bomb. No amount of moralizing afterwards has ever persuaded me to the contrary.

After a trip home and a good vacation, I found that I did not have enough "points" to get out of the army right away. I was unmarried with no children, and so other people had more points that I did, thus I got sent with what remained of the 558th to Camp Hood in Texas, where I spent most of the winter and spring of 1946.

While I was there, a series of amusing events took place. The first one was that I was awarded the Medal of Metz. The Medal of Metz was awarded to those remaining members of the Third Army or the Corps who had participated in the capture of Metz. The mayor of Metz came to Dallas, Texas, to award these medals and an order came out of Army headquarters in Dallas to report on a certain day to receive the medal. The interesting connection was that General Walker presided. He was one of Patton's Corps commanders (who was later killed in Korea in an automobile accident quite similar to the one that killed his patron, General Patton, in Germany). He and the mayor of Metz came down the line of enlisted men and officers, from general down to lieutenant, to give out the Medal of Metz.

Along the way, they ran out of medals, before they reached me. Much to my surprise, accompanying the mayor of Metz was "Colonel O'Neill," whom I had last seen outside of Orleans in July or August of 1944.

When they came past, and the mayor was saying in French that he was sorry they had run out of medals, Colonel O'Neill and I recognized each other and he flung his arms around me and, much to General Walker's disgust, kissed me on both cheeks, and said in French that he was sorry they had run out of medals, whereupon he took a forgère off his shoulder and hung it on me in place of the missing medal.

I thought the forgère was the same thing as it was in our own army, which was either merely a decoration of elite troops or a unit citation, and so I took to wearing it around. About a week later, I was invited to lunch with friends of my parents who lived in New Orleans, and whose name was Benjamin. They were descendants of Judah Benjamin. Judah Benjamin, secretary of war and secretary of state to President Jefferson Davis of the Confederacy, had been a famous and interesting man. They invited me to lunch at Gallctoire's, a famous restaurant in New Orleans. During the lunch, Monsieur Galletoire came over to our table—much to the delight of the Benjamins—and said that Count so-and-so, who always ate at the back of the restaurant and never spoke to anyone, would like to meet me. I went over and presented myself, and, in French, he congratulated me on my decoration. I wasn't wearing anything more remarkable than a purple heart so that I thought it was a little bit odd. However, the Benjamins were very excited about it.

When I got back to Camp Hood, I began to reflect on the meeting with the count and I realized that I was still wearing this forgère. So, a week later I was in Dallas again (you can see how busy I was), and I went in to one of the foremost military stores and asked the owner what this decoration was that I was wearing.

He said, "Where did you get that?" I said, "Never mind where I got it, what is it?"

"Well," he said, "You look a little too young for such a decoration. It's for winning the Croix De Guerre five times."

Colonel O'Neill (or whatever his real name) was old enough, however, and must have won a couple of them in World War I, a couple more in North Africa or French East Asia, and maybe two more in World War II.

From *The History of the 558 Field Artillery Battallion*
Foreword by Colonel Mark F. Conway, FA, Colorado

This copy of the History of the 558th FA Battalion was reproduced by the Military Department, State of Colorado. It was copied from the original history as prepared by Lieutenant Gilbert Hahn upon request of the Historical Section of the Artillery School. Their request was predicated on the basis that the original cadre came from a Colorado unit—the 983rd FA Battalion.

It would be amiss if we failed to mention the great contribution by the State of Utah from whence came the bulk of the fine young men that filled the ranks. The States of Tennessee, Washington, Oregon and California each sent sizable contingents; however, most States were represented by one or two.

In retrospect, I regret that better and more elaborate records were not kept on the activities and exploits of this excellent unit. Our history may appear stilted, modest, and formal, but this cannot detract from the accomplishments of the battalion.

Unrecorded in this history are many deeds of valor and unselfish devotion of soldiers of this battalion. These are recorded in the minds of their comrades.

A word about the author, Lieutenant Gilbert Hahn, who did such a fine job assembling this data from limited material. Lieutenant Hahn graduated from Princeton, and came to the 558th via the Artillery School. His home was Washington, D.C. From the day he arrived in the battalion he exemplified the best traits required of an officer. He was the last of the original officer complement mustered out on deactivation. He is at present

an active young barrister in Washington, D.C. All are indebted to him for
his work on this history.

Denver, Colorado
September 1960

War Stories (continued)

Sometime after D-Day, I landed on Utah Beach with the 558th Field Artillery
Battalion. There was still a war going on at the beaches, and we got stopped
several times. We had not yet been attached to our corps artillery, so Col.
Conway ordered us to dig in while we awaited orders to move inland from
the beach.

To our astonishment, we were greeted by a most unusual sight. Among
the foxholes that were sprouting up, a French farmer was moving along
with a hoe, trying to fill up all the holes that the canoneers were making.

"Hahn," called the colonel. "Come here. You're the only man in this
500-man battalion that speaks any French. Go tell the bastard to stop filling
up the holes."

Ha, French! I had had all of two years of French in prep school. But we
obey orders. I approached the farmer.

"Messieur," I said, "Nous sommes les Americaines, et nous avons venir
se combatre les Boches."

"Ah, oui, oui," he said. And I said, "Notre soldats avoir peur de les
Boche Avions."

"Ah, oui, oui," he said.

I blurted out, "But why the hell are you filling up the foxholes?"

He said, "Les feuilles." I knew that one—the word for *leaf*, but there
were no leaves in sight. We were in a *pine tree* lot.

Finally, he picked up a handful of pine needles and again said "feuilles."
And I finally got it. In Normandy, *leaf* is *pine needle*.

He was, he said, only a poor farmer. He needed the pine needles to
start his fires in the winter. If we left holes in his pine lot, the needles would
fall in, get covered over, and be lost to him.

A good-sized war going on around us and the farmer was concerned
for his pine needles. This was a typical French peasant. They were neutral,
and nothing was going to harm them or interfere with their daily lives. We
were to see this, in different ways, over and over as we moved through
France.

I Nearly Buy It at Metz . . . and Memories of VE Day

On September 12, 1944, I stood, as I've mentioned before, in the town square of Metz, *which* I've mentioned before. There wasn't a German in sight, and the whole Third Army was strung out behind me all the way back to Rheims—and out of gas. The Third Army and I pulled back and went into positions on the West Edge of the Saar-Moselle, where we waited and waited and waited. We had very little ammunition and only enough gasoline to turn over the motors now and again.

We sat there from the middle of September until Thanksgiving, trading artillery fire with the Germans. Then I was moved out of the fire direction center and assigned to a forward observation post where I stayed for forty-five days. We shot at the German horse-drawn artillery. They shot at me. I spent half my time with my glasses on them and the rest crouching in my foxhole while they tried to close me out.

In November, the weather had turned awful, and we began to assault Metz—now fully manned by Germans. Our individual self-propelled guns went forward on the dangerous mission of firing directly into the pill-boxes around Metz. The smaller-sized guns had had no effect, but ours were decisive.

Along with my radio operator, I was moved in toward Metz to help direct our fire. As we pressed through a town named Bourg, the mortars found us. I caught eight to ten pieces of shell fragments (which are different from shrapnel). To my great surprise, I didn't realize I had been wounded until one of my men yelled, "Lieutenant! You've been hit!" Sure enough, he was right. It's strange, but after living in the open, your body gets tougher than you realize, and shock delays the pain—at least it did in my case. I was persuaded to go to the nearest aid station where an obliging medic began probing my holes with a stiff wire, looking for the fragments.

"Patch me up," I said, in true John Wayne style, "and let's get back to it." But they carted me into an ambulance and sent me to a field hospital near Thionville where they operated on me several times to remove the fragments from my stomach and legs, leaving only two. One remains in my ankle to this day, and the other one they missed is in my rib cage. (The orderlies in the field hospital were German prisoners; they passed the bedpans, the medicine, and the rations.)

Thank God for penicillin. Without it I would have been long gone. I recovered some, but they would not send me back to the battalion. Instead, I found myself on a train to Paris. I stayed at the American Hospital there for a short while before they put me and several other wounded soldiers on a plane for England. I wound up at the American Field Hospital at St. Albans. Eventually, as I have already reported, I got back to my battalion.

The day I was wounded was Thanksgiving Day. As I found out later, that was the same day that my grandfather Harry King, whom I loved dearly, died back home in Washington. I've often wondered if he died in my place.

Before I went back to my battalion, I got several days off to go into London, however, where I had several experiences that I can still recall quite easily.

I went to the Windmill theater, the English version of an American burlesque house, where the nude girls were—by order of the lord chamberlin—not allowed to move, and stood as if they were statues. Not so the streetwalkers of London, who lingered in front of alleys or mews with their key on a long chain. They twirled the chains and invited your "patronage." When refused, they would call out, "What's the matter, Yank— Savin' yer money for breakfast?"

On VE day, I was in Hyde Park, part of the huge, happy crowd that surged, with me right up front, under the balcony of Buckingham Palace. There, on the balcony, appeared King George VI, and the queen (100 years old as I write this!), Winston and Clementine Churchill, and the future queen Elizabeth and her younger sister, Margaret. It was totally exciting!

Moe Berg and the Atomic Bomb

My brief participation in the war against Japan made me a lifelong lover of the atomic bomb. After my war against the Germans and my stay in the hospitals after my wounding in the Metz campaign in November 1944, I was returned to duty, rejoining my old battalion, the 558 Field Artillery, then in the environs of Marseilles. It was getting ready to be combat-loaded and transported to Japan. The army wanted our self-propelled 155-mm guns for direct firing into caves in Japan. (Elsewhere in these notes, I have described the hazards involved in this direct fire work.) With separate loading ammunition, which requires the exposure of powder bags to return fire from machine guns and mortars, this activity can be suicidal. Having survived one war in France and Germany, I was sure that my luck would run out when we had a go at the Japs.

The highlight of my stay occurred one evening at the amphitheater in Arles (or Nimes) watching the Paris Opera Company perform *Aida* spectacularly, elephants and all. Soon thereafter, we loaded ourselves on a troopship bound for Japan across the South Atlantic and through the Panama Canal.

As we went through the straits of Gibraltar, we received news of the dropping of the atomic bomb on Hiroshima. It is fair to say that none of us had any idea what an atomic bomb was, nor could we conceive the vast destruction that it caused. In the South Atlantic, we received the report of the second bomb at Nagasaki—and news that the war with Japan was over! Over the loudspeaker the captain said, "Watch the wake. We are turning northwest and heading for Newark and home."

What little that conveyed was all good news. We were going home, the war was over, and there would be no combat landing on the beaches of Japan, no direct lay firing into caves.

I remained in the army for another year at Camp Hood in Texas, waiting to be released to civilian life. I got home in 1946 and spent my time before going to Yale Law School in the fall working as a clerk on the staff of the Republican Policy Committee in the U.S. Senate. The committee, which was chaired by Senator Robert Taft of Ohio, prepared policy issues for what was then the minority party in the Senate. The staff director was a Mr. Robert Smith. An extraordinary man, he was married to Betty Smith, the author of *A Tree Grows in Brooklyn*. Mr. Smith also had a permanent home outside of New Haven, and I saw him from time to time while I was at Yale.

One of the rather odd things we did was to oppose the creation of the National Science Foundation that had been proposed by the Democratic administration to organize science research in peacetime, similar to what had been done during the war. We started with this premise: There was a translation of a Russian version of the National Science Act that appeared to be almost word for word with the administration's proposal, and the thinking was that if it was Russian, it must be a bad thing.

In what I guess was an effort to persuade us to come off of our opposition, a group of the bill's supporters invited Bob Smith and me to a reception at a large house used for such meetings at the bottom of Cleveland Avenue. The featured speaker of the afternoon was the eminent Dr. Vannever Bush, who stressed the importance of the National Science Foundation as a form of protection for our nation. He told the following story.

During the winter of 1944–45, General Bedell Smith summoned Dr. Bush to Rheims, where General Eisenhower had his headquarters. When Bush arrived, he was told that Ike's headquarters, being aware of the Manhattan Project to build an atomic bomb, assumed the Germans were also working on the same thing. General Eisenhower wanted to know how soon the Germans would have a workable bomb. He wanted to postpone his final push into Germany until the spring, thereby avoiding some 100,000 American casualties. But if the Germans might have the bomb by the spring, then he was prepared to make his final attack that winter and sustain the 100,000 casualties. Dr. Bush was able to assure the general that he was confident the Germans were too far away from perfecting the bomb to interfere with the general's plan to wait until the spring for the final attack on Germany.

In his talk, Dr. Bush explained that by citing certain work that the Germans were doing in Norway with "heavy water," he and his fellow scientists could tell how far along, in comparison with the Americans, the Germans were. Translation: They were a long way from a perfected bomb. The Americans had been working with heavy water for a long time. What he did not talk about—though I'm sure he knew of it—was the role played by a man named Moe Berg.

Moe Berg had been a second-string catcher for the Washington Senators before the war, when I was a child and a great fan of the Senators. A competent catcher who hung on in the American League, Berg was by no means a star. He was, however, a genius with a gift for learning foreign languages. (Casey Stengel once said, "Moe Berg speaks six languages, but he can't hit in any of them.")

Moe Berg, a Jew of course, had attended Princeton, where he'd been captain of the baseball team. He wanted to play professional baseball, but his father thought this was not a nice thing for a Jewish boy to do. Still, Moe persisted.

Because of his language skills and other accomplishments, Berg had apparently become a spy for American intelligence. While in Japan, touring with an American All-Star team, he was reputed to have taken rooftop photos of Tokyo that were supposedly used by General Doolittle in his raid on Tokyo early in the war.

I came across the Moe Berg atomic bomb story in this way. Because someone asked about my great uncle Phil King, a famous quarterback at Princeton around 1900 and Grantland Rice's All-American quarterback choice, wanting to check my facts I went to the Library of Congress to look up the career of Uncle Phil. I found several books on famous American Jewish athletes in which Uncle Phil was prominently mentioned. In one of them, a chapter about Moe Berg caught my eye.

According to the book, during the war, Berg was enlisted by the OSS (Office of Strategic Services, the forerunner of the CIA) because of his language skills, was sent to Albert Einstein to bone up on nuclear physics, and then, having been given a gun, was shipped to Switzerland. There he was to make contact with Werner Heisenberger, a German physicist who was a key person in the German atomic program and who was in Switzerland to deliver a lecture. Moe Berg's job was to attend the lecture, find out how far along the German program was in accomplishing a workable atomic bomb, and, if it appeared from what Heisenberger said that he and his German colleagues were close to achieving a workable bomb, he was to shoot him! If it was a long way off, he was to say, "hello and goodbye," but if the reverse were true, he was to kill him. Apparently, Berg reported that the German bomb program was not far enough along to be taken seriously, thus it was not necessary for him to shoot Heisenberger.

In later years, I became friends with General Bill Quinn, who'd been a distinguished officer in World War II. Bill Quinn was put in charge of Army National Intelligence following the end of the OSS and before the creation of the CIA. The article about Moe Berg mentioned that Bill Quinn's agency had given Berg its highest award for services during the war. Was this for the work he'd done on A-Bomb intelligence and his eminently useful report submitted to Dr. Bush and passed on by him to General Bedell Smith?

Bryce Bowmar and the Real War

My very good friend Bryce Bowmar died in September 2001. Fortunately, in 1999, he and I had traveled to Carson City, Nevada, to attend a reunion of the 558 Field Artillery, the unit in which we had served—under Gen. George Patton—in World War II. We were both lieutenants, but with different assignments. Bryce had been the executive officer in charge of C Battery's guns, and I was the gunnery and fire control officer at headquarters, though I often served as forward observer as well.

At the reunion, we talked as we always did, "swapping lies" about the war and our close brushes with death. But we also both mentioned the funny and the sad things that happen to young men in war.

I told Bryce I had been reading a book about the battle of Stalingrad that detailed the Stalingrad campaign, the most critical battle of the Russian campaign. When he expressed an interest in reading it himself, I told him I would send it to him, and I later did.

A few weeks later I got a call from California. It was Bryce, calling from his home there to tell me how much he had enjoyed the book and to thank me. Then, after a pause, he said, "You know, Gil, that really was war. What you and I were doing was just playing at war."

About the Author
ℰℭ

Gilbert Hahn, Jr. is a member of the Hahn Shoe family and a lifelong resident of the District of Columbia. He graduated from Princeton University and Yale Law School; was a wounded and decorated field artillery forward observer in General George Patton's Third Army during World War II; and served as chairman of the District of Columbia City Council from 1969 to 1972. A Washington lawyer for over fifty years, he has had a lifetime interest in the welfare of the District of Columbia and his fellow Washingtonians. Mr. Hahn has been married fifty years to the beautiful Margo Hess Hahn, of the Baltimore Hess Shoe family; she is a noted collector of Pop Art as well as a gourmet chef and private cooking school teacher. They have three children and five grandchildren.